COOL CAREERS WITHOUT COLLEGE FOR
PEOPLE
WHO LOVE
TO FIX
THINGS

COOL CAREERS WITHOUT COLLEGE FOR
PEOPLE
WHO LOVE
TO FIX
THINGS

LINDA BICKERSTAFF

The Rosen Publishing Group, Inc.
New York

Dedicated to a good friend, Stu Otis (1928–2002),
direct descendant of Elisha Otis, inventor of the first safety elevator.
Genes ran true from him to Stu.

Published in 2004 by The Rosen Publishing Group, Inc.
29 East 21st Street, New York, NY 10010

Library of Congress Cataloging-in-Publication Data

Bickerstaff, Linda.
Cool careers without college for people who love to fix things/ by
Linda Bickerstaff.— 1st ed.
   p. cm. — (Cool careers without college)
Summary: Explores the job descriptions, education and training
requirements, salary, and outlook predictions for twelve careers that
focus on repair work and do not require a college education.
Includes bibliographical references and index.
ISBN 0-8239-3788-7
1. Repairing—Vocational guidance—Juvenile literature. 2. Repairing
trades—Vocational guidance—Juvenile literature. [1. Repairing
trades—Vocational guidance. 2. Building trades—Vocational guidance.
3. Vocational guidance.] I. Title. II. Series.
TT151 .B53 2002
690'.023—dc21

2002012101

Manufactured in the United States of America

CONTENTS

Introduction 7

1 Auto Body Repair
  Technician 9

2 Aviation Technologist 19

3 Concrete Mason 30

4 Roofer 41

5 Lineworker 52

6 Elevator Constructor
  and Repairer 62

7 Historic Preservationist 73

8 Motorcycle Mechanic 84

9 Horologist 95

10 Heating, Ventilation,
   Air-Conditioning, and
   Refrigeration
   (HVACR) Technician 106

11 Computer Repair
   Technician 117

12 Upholsterer 128

Glossary 137

Index 140

INTRODUCTION

Do you like to tinker? Were you one of those kids who dismantled clocks to see what made them work? Do you want to learn how to pound the dents out of cars' bodies or fix computers? Does a career built around fixing things sound cool? If so, this book's for you!

There are hundreds of employers looking for people who are curious, who work well with their hands, and who get a lot of satisfaction from making things work. The careers described in this book do not require traditional college degrees, but almost all require that you graduate from high school or obtain a general equivalency diploma (GED). Specific training for the chosen career is then obtained in trade schools, vocational or technical institutions, one- or two-year community college programs, by apprenticeships, by distance-learning programs, or by do-it-yourself home study courses.

Gender bias is rapidly disappearing in most fields. Many of the careers discussed here, however, are considered non-traditional for women because fewer than 25 percent of workers in the field are women. Choose a career based on your interests, your abilities, and your ambitions rather than on what is considered traditional. Choose what you want to do, then go for it!

1

AUTO BODY REPAIR TECHNICIAN

The number of vehicles on America's roads increases daily, as do the number of vehicular accidents. Because a car or truck is the second most expensive investment a person makes in a lifetime (after buying a house), every effort is made to repair damage sustained in an accident. According to the Automotive Service Association

An auto body repair technician buffs a car to remove scratches and grime. Buffing can keep a car looking brand new for decades and can also help prevent rust.

(ASA), an organization of owners and managers of automotive businesses, more than $30 billion is spent yearly on automotive collision repairs. Auto body repair technicians, working with auto mechanics, can take a damaged vehicle and make it good as new or maybe even better!

There are several personal characteristics that are common to auto body repair technicians. They are creative and artistic and have a good eye for shape and color. They enjoy working with their hands and have a lot of mechanical aptitude. Above all else, they are passionate about cars! If this description fits you perfectly, give serious consideration to becoming an auto body technician.

Job Description

Auto body technicians may specialize in structural repairs, automotive painting, or automotive glass replacement, or may train in all areas of auto body repair. No two damaged vehicles are exactly alike. This presents a special challenge to the auto body technician, who must develop a unique plan for the repair of each vehicle. The job may require that bent structures be straightened. Dents may need to be removed and crushed parts replaced. Once repairs are made, all or part of the vehicle will need to be repainted and refinished. Because modern cars are made of more than steel, auto body technicians work with fiberglass, plastics, and aluminum and will soon need to know how to work with carbon fiber materials.

Education and Training

Some high schools offer introductory or basic repair courses while other high schools, which specialize in technical training, offer the same course work as a technical college. At a minimum, a high school student should take English, basic high school math, auto shop, and metal shop. The addition of algebra and basic physics to these courses would be helpful.

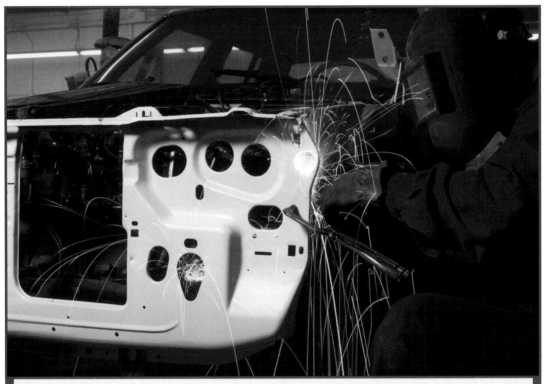

This welder repairs the body of an automobile. Because many automobiles will be driven for hundreds of thousands of miles, it is important that all the body welds be solid.

Almost all specialty training programs require that applicants be high school graduates or have a GED.

Post-secondary school training for a career as an auto body repair technician may be obtained at vocational schools, private trade schools, and community colleges (see sidebar on page 14). Completion of two-year programs in these institutions will lead to an associate of science or an associate of applied science degree. These schools may also offer one-year programs leading to a certificate of completion.

Apprenticeship programs are also available, especially in Canada. In these programs, auto body technician trainees receive on-the-job training (OJT), for which they are paid, while working with fully trained technicians. Classroom work at the training site or an affiliated school is also required. Apprenticeship programs are not plentiful in the United States at the present time. Because of a shortage of qualified technicians, more programs are being developed. Many of these are partnerships between educational institutions and automobile and auto parts manufacturers.

It usually takes three to five years of OJT to become skilled in all aspects of auto body repair. Formal training may decrease the amount of work experience needed to become skilled. Certification by the National Institute for Automotive Service Excellence (ASE) adds to an auto body technician's credentials. The institute offers four examinations for auto body technicians. After successful completion of all four exams, a technician becomes an ASE master collision repair technician. Automotive body repair technicians must retake the exam every five years to retain certification. Continuing education is required in order to keep up with technological advances.

Job Options

According to an I-Car Education Foundation survey, the demand for auto body repair technicians is at an all-time

Types of Training

Diana Fell, in an article featured on the Web site www.careerexplorer.net, compares training received in a vocational school with that obtained in a community or junior college. She says, "Generally speaking, colleges (two- and four-year schools) specialize in academic learning and theory. Vocational or trade schools often specialize in applied skills." She goes on to say, "When you want to learn how to physically do something, particularly when it involves your hands in some way, look into what vocational or trade schools can offer." She admits that there is a lot of crossover in the training provided in each type of school and that the only way to see what is available is to contact all the schools in your area.

high. There is actually a shortage of quality entry-level technicians. The Bureau of Labor Statistics (BLS), a branch of the Department of Labor, says that opportunities are best for people with formal training, and that job opportunities will increase as the number of motor vehicles increases.

Most collision repair technicians work for shops specializing in auto body repair and painting or for auto or truck dealers. Others work for trucking or car rental companies who maintain large fleets of vehicles. Nearly 20 percent of all auto body technicians are self-employed.

Salary and Benefits

Although there is a wide variety of salaries in the auto body repair field, salaries have increased steadily since 1995. According to the I-Car Education Foundation survey, the average annual income for all collision repair technicians is $37,189. Salaries range from $23,000 to $66,000 per year. The BLS reports a similar range of salaries.

The collision repair industry does not offer a consistent level of benefits. According to the I-Car Education Foundation survey, only 80 percent of employers offer paid vacations, 60 percent offer health insurance, and 50 percent offer life insurance and some type of retirement plan. Almost 15 percent offer no benefits.

Pros and Cons

The automotive repair business is not sensitive to changes in economic conditions. As a result, auto body technicians are rarely laid off. Since auto body work is not done on an emergency basis, the number of hours worked a week tends to be consistent. This allows for adequate time off to pursue other interests. One other pro, and a big one, is that auto body technician skills are transferable. If you want or need to move to another city, state, or country, your skills will be in demand there as well.

On the other side of the coin, technicians often work in awkward or cramped positions in very noisy shops. While serious accidents are unusual, cuts from sharp metal edges, burns from torches and heated metals, and skin problems from the use of paints and solvents are relatively common. The pros though, far outweigh the cons in this profession.

FOR MORE INFORMATION

ASSOCIATIONS

Automotive Service and Repair Association
Box 53122 Glenora PO
Edmonton, AB T5N 4A8
Canada
(780) 463-9292 or (800) 282-9909
Web site: http://www.asra-alberta.ab.ca
This association provides mechanical and collision repair directories and other information to consumers, technicians, and employers. Some job opportunities are listed here.

National Automotive Technicians Education Foundation
101 Blue Seal Drive, Suite 101
Leesburg, VA 20175
(703) 669-6650
Web site: http://www.natef.org

Established in 1983, this foundation evaluates technician-training programs according to standards developed by the automotive industry.

National Institute for Automotive Service Excellence

101 Blue Seal Drive, Suite 101
Leesburg, VA 20175
(877) 669–6600
Web site: http://www.asecert.org
This institute was founded in 1972 to improve the quality of automotive service and repair through the voluntary testing and certification of automotive technicians.

WEB SITES

Bureau of Labor Statistics
http://www.bls.gov
A directory of occupations is available on this Web site.

CCar-CareerLink
http://www.ccar-careerlink.org
The Coordination Committee on Automotive Repairs of the National Auto Body Council provides information on this Web site to assist students who are considering a career in the auto body industry.

The I-Car Education Foundation
http://www.i-car.com
The foundation is dedicated to attracting quality, entry-level candidates. It offers people assistance in preparing for careers in the collision industry.

National Auto Body Council
http://www.autobodycouncil.org
For people who work in the auto body industry.

Society of Collision Repair Specialists
http://www.scrs.com
This is the Web site of an organization committed to expanding the future of the collision repair industry.

BOOKS

Chilton's Guide to Auto Body Repair. Pittsburgh, PA: Chilton/Haynes Publishing, 1990.

Pfanstiehl, John et. al. *Automotive Paint Handbook: Paint Technology for Auto Enthusiasts and Body Shop Professionals*. New York: The Berkley Publishing Group, 1998.

Rhone, L., and David Yates. *Total Auto Body Repair*. New York: Glencoe McGraw-Hill, 1990.

Scharff, Robert, James Duffy, and Michael Crandell. *Motor Auto Body Repair: Student Technicians' Manual*. Albany, NY: Delmar Publishing, 1997.

Toboldt, William, and Terry Richardson. *Auto Body Repairing and Refinishing*. Tinley Park, IL: Goodhard-Willcox Co., 1993.

PERIODICALS

The following magazines may be purchased at your local newsstand or auto parts store. They are also available by subscription:

AutoWeek
Automotive Week Publishing Co, Inc.
P.O. Box 3495
Wayne, NJ 07474-3495
Web site: http://www.autoweek.com

Car and Driver
Hachette Magazines, Inc.
1633 Broadway
New York, NY 10019

Motor Trend
Primedia Magazines
Web site: http://www.motortrend.com

2

AVIATION TECHNOLOGIST

Have you ever heard of Charles Taylor? Probably not, unless you are a Wright brothers buff or an aviation mechanic. Taylor was the first aircraft mechanic in the United States. He helped design, build, and maintain Orville and Wilbur Wright's 1903 Flyer.

An advisory circular distributed by the Federal Aviation

Although pilots get most of the attention, mechanics are the ones who make sure that planes are safe to fly.

Administration (FAA) describes aviation maintenance as a dynamic career field. It is dynamic in more than one sense of the word. Constantly changing, it is a field that deals with the dynamism of force and energy. If you are a person who enjoys dynamic challenges, who recognizes that learning is a lifelong process, and who gets goose bumps when a B-2 flies over, put aviation technology on your career short list!

Job Description

The U.S. Department of Labor's *Occupational Handbook* says that aircraft mechanics, or aviation technologists, are responsible for keeping aircraft in peak operating condition. They do this by providing scheduled maintenance, making repairs, and completing numerous inspections required by the FAA.

There are strict schedules of preventive maintenance for aircraft. Engines, for instance, are removed from planes, completely dismantled, and reassembled after an established number of hours of flight. Technologists use precision instruments to measure parts for wear and X-rays to look for cracks or other defects not visible to the eye. After making repairs and replacing parts, technologists test all equipment to make sure everything works properly.

Aviation technologists may specialize in one of three fields or may qualify in all three. Power plant technologists work on engines and, to a limited degree, on propellers. Airframe technologists work on the body parts of an aircraft except the avionic, or instrument systems, engines, and propellers. Many aviation mechanics are qualified as both power plant and airframe technologists, and are called A&P technologists.

Mechanics who work with aircraft navigation equipment, radios, and other communications equipment are called avionics technicians. They also work on weather radar systems and the computers that control the primary functions of the aircraft. This field is becoming progressively more specialized as a result of rapid advancements in the

The planes in Canada's Aviation Museum are no longer being built, making it difficult to find parts for them. As a result, mechanics take extra pains to make sure nothing goes wrong with their aircraft. Sometimes they are able to find pieces of old planes that they can use for repairs.

use of computer-controlled systems in aircraft. While it is possible for an aviation technologist to train as an A&P tech as well as an avionics tech, it is becoming very difficult to remain proficient in both areas.

Education and Training

Although it is not specifically required to obtain FAA certification, a high school diploma or GED is very important in gaining admission to an aviation technology school. High school courses that are recommended include English, industrial arts, drafting, auto shop, electric shop, metal shop, physics, and math including algebra. Calculus would also be very helpful.

To obtain FAA certification as a power plant technician or an airframe technician, a person must be at least eighteen years old and be able to read, write, and understand English. The candidate must have eighteen months (160 hours per month) of on-the-job training under the supervision of a qualified technician, or be a graduate of an FAA-approved aviation maintenance technology school. The candidate must then pass written, oral, and practical exams. To qualify for certification as an A&P technician, thirty months of training are needed.

Because of the increasing complexity of aviation technology, most technologists receive their training in FAA-approved aviation technology schools. Courses may last from two to three years, and at the end of training, a student may receive an associate of science or an associate of applied science degree. Some schools also offer airframe and power plant certificates after two years of training. Most A&P courses require 2,000 to 2,100 hours of class and lab work. Avionics technology courses are of similar length. After completion of training, candidates must take and pass FAA exams.

The armed services also provide excellent training programs in aviation technology. These skills can be translated into civilian jobs when one leaves or retires from the military.

The Birth of Avionics

The career profile in the *Princeton Review* says that avionics developed with the rise of modern warfare. "The number of electronic devices used in navigation, control, maintenance and flight multiplied by a factor of 100 between the World War II B-29 and the current B-58 supersonic bomber." One manufacturer of avionics equipment said that by 1999, avionics technology was turning over once every year. The three most significant advances that are sustaining these giant technological steps are digital electronics, the capability for satellite communication, and onboard maintenance computers. Flight crews, who have previously relied on voice communication, will need to become adept at interpreting electronic displays. James F. Pendergrass, Spartan School of Aeronautics, believes that proficiency in playing video games will be an asset to flight crews and avionics technicians of the future.

Job Options

According to the FAA, the long-term outlook for employment in aviation technology is bright. Scheduled airlines employ over 50,000 aviation technologists, and there are another 37,000 employed in general aviation jobs. The U.S.

government also employs civilian aircraft mechanics and avionics technologists to work on military aircraft and for the FAA.

Employment opportunities are likely to be best with smaller commuter and regional airlines or in general aviation jobs in FAA repair stations, servicing private or corporate aircraft.

While major airlines have been adversely affected by the terrorist acts of September 11, 2001, the true impact on aviation technology as a whole, at this writing, is still unknown.

Salary and Benefits

The following data on salaries is supplied by the FAA in its advisory circular on aviation technology.

Yearly Salaries (40 hr/wk)	A&P Tech		Avionics Tech	
	Starting	After 5 years	Starting	After 5 years
Major Carriers	$20,000 to $27,000	$35,000 to $40,000	$25,000 to $30,000	$38,000 to $48,000
General Aviation	$18,000 to $24,000	$23,000 to $30,000	$22,000 to $25,000	$28,000 to $35,000

Most technicians in the general aviation field believe that the disadvantages of their lower salaries are out-weighed by advantages associated with working in smaller towns for smaller employers. These include a lower cost of living, a better quality of life, and much less job stress.

Benefit packages vary from employer to employer as do shift, weekend, and overtime work. General aviation jobs usually offer fewer benefits than do jobs with major carriers.

Pros and Cons

Aviation technology is an exciting career choice. Dreams created by science fiction writers a few decades ago are now becoming reality. Advancements in computer technology, satellite communication technology, materials technology, space exploration, and many other allied fields ensure that aviation technologists will not get bored with the job. A person who is curious and willing to keep learning will have a wonderful and well-paid career in aviation.

There is little if any room for error in aviation technology. Lives depend on a job well done. Because of this and because of tight airline schedules, aviation technology can be very stressful. It can also be physically demanding, requiring climbing, stooping, kneeling, and some heavy lifting. Although most work is done in hangars or other areas where weather is not a factor, some work may be done outdoors where adverse weather can add to stressful situations.

Air travel is affected by the economic climate. In bad times, people don't fly as much. Airlines may be forced to lay off maintenance employees until business picks up.

FOR MORE INFORMATION

ASSOCIATIONS

Aircraft Mechanics Fraternal Association
67 Water Street, Suite 208A
Laconia, NH 03246
(800) 520-2632
Web site: http:// www.amfanatl.org
Craft oriented, this independent aviation union is committed to elevating the professional standing of aviation maintenance technologists.

American Institute of Aeronautics and Astronautics
1801 Alexander Bell Drive, Suite 500
Reston, VA 20191-4344
(703) 264-7500 or (800) 639-AIAA (2422)
Web site: http://www.aiaa.org
This institute is dedicated to advancing the art, science, and technology of aeronautics and astronautics.

Professional Aviation Maintenance Association
1707 H Street, Suite 700
Washington, DC 20006-3915
(202) 730-0260
Web site: http://www.pama.org
The mission of this organization is to enhance professionalism and

recognition of aviation maintenance technicians through communication and education. It also advocates continuous improvement in aviation safety.

WEB SITES

AVJobs.com
http://www.avjobs.com

AviationNow.com
http://www.aviationnow.com

Canadian Aviation Maintenance Council Careers
http://www.camc.ca

BOOKS

Crane, Dale. *Aviation Mechanics Handbook*. New Castle, WA: Aviation Supplies and Academics, Inc., 2000.

Kayton, Myron, ed. *Avionic Navigation Systems*. New York: John Wiley and Sons, 1997.

Reda, Helmut, ed. *Because I Fly: A Collection of Aviation Poetry*. New York: McGraw-Hill, 2001.

Reithmaier, Larry, ed. *Standard Aircraft Handbook*. New York: McGraw-Hill, 1999.

Wright, Wilbur, ed. *The Papers of Wilbur and Orville Wright, Including the Chanute-Wright Papers*. New York: McGraw-Hill, 1972.

PERIODICALS

Aviation History
Web site: https://store.primediamags.com/subscribe/aviationhistory/G1LHN1
Published by Primedia Magazines, this magazine is available by subscription.

Aviation Week and Space Technology
Web site: http://www.aviationnow.com

Overhaul & Maintenance
http://www.aviationnow.com

DVD

Superior Airpower **(2000)**
This DVD was produced by Goldhill Home Media.

3

CONCRETE MASON

What do the Pyramids in Egypt, the Coliseum in Rome, and the London sewer system have in common with the sidewalk in front of your house? Nothing? Guess again! Each was built using an amazing material called cement. The Egyptians used a mixture of lime and gypsum as mortar between the huge stones of the Pyramids. In Rome, volcanic

Did You Know?

Thomas Edison, usually associated with the invention of the light bulb and the phonograph, was a pioneer in the cement industry. In 1902 he introduced a rotating kiln that was 150 feet (45.7 meters) long. The increased length of the kiln improved mixing of the components and led to a more uniform product. Kilns today may be as long as 500 feet (152.4 meters).

ash from Mt. Vesuvius, called pozzolana, was mixed with lime to produce a cement that would harden under water. The most common type of cement used today, and the cement used to build the sewers of London, is portland cement. It was developed in 1824 by Joseph Aspdin, a bricklayer in London. He named it portland cement because its color reminded him of stone found on the Isle of Portland off the coast of Britain.

Today's portland cement is a precise mixture of lime and other calcium compounds, silica, aluminum oxide, and iron oxide. Proper proportions of these ingredients are mixed together in a kiln and heated to very high temperatures (2,700 to 3,000° F; 1,482 to 1,649° C). As water and carbon dioxide are driven off in the heating process, the components are chemically changed. The end product is called clinker. Clinker is then ground into a very fine powder—portland cement.

Ninety-five percent of all cement is used to make concrete. Concrete is 6 percent air, 11 percent portland cement, 41 percent gravel or crushed stone (coarse aggregate), 26 percent sand (fine aggregate), and 16 percent water. These ingredients are mixed in concrete mixers (not cement mixers!), transported to construction sites, then poured or cast to make a building, repair a highway, or fix the cracks in your sidewalk.

People who work with concrete are called concrete masons. Without their skills and their ability to see the potential uses for concrete, most of the construction in the world today would cease.

Job Description

Concrete masons first set the forms that will hold the concrete. Forms or molds must be the correct depth, have the right pitch, and be properly aligned before the concrete can be poured or cast. Concrete masons supervise workers who spread the concrete throughout the forms. They level the freshly placed concrete with the top of the forms. The edges of the concrete are "finished" with slightly rounded edges to

This concrete mason pours a road bed in California. Concrete masons must be very attentive to their work—if a concrete mixture is incorrect it will not be structurally sound when it hardens.

The Popularity of Concrete

Concrete is the world's most widely used building material. Globally, almost 5 billion cubic yards, or 1.25 billion tons, of cement are made yearly.

prevent chipping or cracking. Concrete masons then make joints or grooves in the concrete at specific intervals to help control cracking. They use power tools and hand trowels to smooth out the surface.

Concrete masons must have a thorough knowledge of concrete's characteristics so that they can determine what is happening with the concrete and take measures that will prevent problems during the curing process. If the mason is working on a repair job, it may be necessary to color the concrete with dye in order to match existing concrete. On concrete surfaces that will remain exposed after the forms are stripped—such as columns, ceilings, or wall panels—concrete masons cut away high spots and loose concrete. They fill all indentations with portland cement paste and smooth the surface with a rubbing Carborundum stone. They apply a final coat of rich portland cement mixture, and, using a coarse cloth, rub the concrete to a uniform finish.

Education and Training

High school courses that will be helpful in this field are English, shop, mathematics, blueprint reading, and mechanical drawing. A high school diploma or GED is strongly recommended.

Concrete masons learn their trade through on-the-job training, starting as helpers with concrete construction crews, or through two- to three-year apprenticeship programs. These programs are usually sponsored by local unions and contractors. Apprentices receive 144 hours of classroom instruction each year in applied mathematics, blueprint reading, layout work, cost estimating, and safety. A final written test and a physical exam may be required at the end of the apprenticeship.

Job Options

Most concrete masons work for concrete contractors on projects such as highway repair, bridge building and repair, shopping malls, and other large construction jobs. Fewer than 10 percent of concrete masons are self-employed, and they usually specialize in small jobs.

The Bureau of Labor Statistics reports that employment in concrete masonry will grow more slowly than the average for all occupations through the year 2006. Gene Vineyard at Concrete Careers, a recruiting firm for the concrete industry, does not agree. He says, "From our perspective as a recruiter

These workers are fixing the Oakland Bay Bridge, which partially collapsed during the San Francisco earthquake of 1989. Laboring around the clock, crews managed to repair the bridge in twenty-eight days.

for the concrete industry, there is a major shortage of good folks in all aspects of the masonry industry, from masons to people in manufacturing. It looks like there is going to be an even greater shortage in the future."

The demand for concrete masons will rise as the population and the economy grow. The increasing use of concrete as a building material will add to the demand. Repairing and rebuilding the thousands of miles of highway that are now wearing out will also require large numbers of concrete masons.

Salary and Benefits

The Bureau of Labor Statistics reports that the median weekly salary for a full-time concrete mason is $467. The range of salaries is $286 to $823 per week. Average hourly earnings, including benefits, for concrete masons who belong to a union range between $15.10 and $45.84 per hour. Non-union workers generally have lower salaries and fewer benefits. Apprentices receive 50 to 60 percent of the rate paid to experienced workers.

Once concrete has been cast, the job must be finished. This frequently requires that concrete masons work over-time for which they receive additional pay.

Gene Vineyard says, "Salaries would be from $20,000 to $50,000 (per year) and beyond."

Pros and Cons

A good deal of artistry is involved in concrete masonry, especially in the blending of concrete colors for repair jobs, and in the mixing of dyes for colored concrete in new construction. Concrete masons derive a lot of satisfaction from knowing that if they do their jobs well, the construction or repair will last for years. Concrete, after all, gets harder with age and is therefore able to stand the ravages of time.

Concrete work is fast-paced and strenuous. It requires a lot of bending and kneeling. Most of the work is done out-doors, so weather may be a factor. Work is usually stopped during very cold or rainy weather.

Working with uncured concrete can lead to chemical burns, so workers must wear protective clothing, including kneepads and gloves. Rubber boots are also a necessity when working in wet concrete.

FOR MORE INFORMATION

ASSOCIATIONS

Associated Builders and Contractors
1300 N. Seventeenth Street, Suite 800
Rosslyn, VA 22209
(703) 812-2000
Web site: http://www.abc.org
This association represents building contractors, subcontractors, and suppliers.

Cement Association of Canada
1500-60 Queen Street
Ottawa, ON K1P 5Y7
Canada

(613) 236-9471
Web site: http://www.cpca.ca
The Cement Association of Canada represents Canadian cement workers. Its Web site has excellent information on cement.

National Concrete Masonry Association
13750 Sunrise Valley Drive
Herndon, VA 20171-3499
(703) 713-1900
Web site: http://www.ncma.org
This national trade association, which represents the concrete masonry industry, provides general information about it.

Portland Cement Association
5420 Old Orchard Road
Skokie, IL 60077
(847) 966-6200
Web site: http://www.portcement.org
Representing cement manufacturers, this association offers information about the manufacture and use of cement.

WEB SITES

Associated Builders and Contractors—Kentucky/Louisiana Chapter
http://www.kyanaabc.com/concrete.htm
There are good discussions about careers in concrete on this Web site, provided by the Kentucky and Louisiana chapter of the Associated Builders and Contractors.

Coalition for Quality Concrete Flatwork
http://www.flatwork.org
The goal of this coalition is to ease the shortage of concrete finishers and improve educational opportunities for people already in the field.

ConcreteCareers.com
http://www.concretecareers.com
This is the Web site of a recruiter for the concrete industry.

National Center for Construction Education and Research
http://www.nccer.org
This foundation was created to address the issue of workforce shortage and to standardize course work for training programs.

BOOKS

Black and Decker: The Complete Guide to Home Masonry. Minnetonka, Mn: Creative Publishing International, 2000.
This book deals with how to solve masonry problems that may occur at home.

Dobrowolski, Joseph, and Joseph Waddell, eds. *Concrete Construction Handbook*, 4th ed. Columbus, OH: McGraw-Hill, 1996.
Considered the bible of the industry, this book covers an entire range of subjects on modern technology and advanced practices in concrete construction.

Nolan, Ken. *Masonry and Concrete Construction*, Rev. ed. Carlsbad, CA: Craftsman Book Co., 2000.

Schwartz. Max. *Basic Concrete Engineering For Builders*. Carlsbad, CA: Craftsman Book Co., 2001.

U.S. Department of the Army, eds. *Concrete Masonry and Brickwork: A Practical Guide for Home Owners and Small Builders*. Mineola, NY: Dover Publishing, 1999.

PERIODICALS

Concrete Construction
Concrete Producer
Masonry Construction
These magazines are available by subscription.
Hanley-Wood Regional Office
426 South Westgate Street
Addison, IL 60101
(630) 543-0870
Web site: http://www.hanley-wood.com/

4

ROOFER

Drip, drip, splash, plink! Sound familiar? If you've ever had a leak in your roof on a rainy day, it does. While roofers are an integral part of the new construction industry, repair and reroofing are the mainstay of the roofing business. Economic slowdowns may bring new construction to a halt, but there are plenty of old roofs out there just waiting to be fixed! Roofing is a career

that provides steady employment and better-than-average salaries, so if you enjoy working outdoors, have a good sense of balance, and enjoy working with a team, roofing may be for you.

Job Description

The primary reason to repair or reroof a building is to prevent water damage to the structure and to the contents of the building. There are two general categories of roofs: flat roofs and pitched, or sloped, roofs. Commercial buildings, schools, and other very large buildings tend to have flat or only slightly sloped roofs. In their original construction, insulation is laid on the plywood roof decking. This is covered with bitumen, one of the substances left after petroleum is refined into gasoline. The bitumen is heated to allow it to flow over the insulation. Several layers of roofing felt, saturated in bitumen, are then applied in overlapping layers called plies. Hot bitumen is spread between layers to seal seams and insure that they are watertight. The top layer is then glazed to a smooth finish or embedded with gravel for a rough finish.

This roofer puts shingles on the roof of a new house. Roofers always have to be focused on the job, as loose shingles can cause them to fall and injure themselves.

Repair of this type of roof may be as simple as applying another layer of bitumen or may require that the entire process be repeated. Many flat roofs are now being covered with a single layer of waterproof rubber or thermoplastic, which is held in place with adhesives or mechanical fasteners.

Sloped roof decks, which are usually constructed of solid plywood, are first covered with heavy, asphalt-saturated black paper. This is covered with asphalt or wood shingles, slate, ceramic tile, concrete tile, or some type of metal roofing. Wherever two rooflines meet, or are pierced by vent pipes or chimneys, metal or shingle strips called flashings are nailed or cemented over the joints to make them watertight. As a last step, all exposed nail heads are coated with roofing cement or caulking to prevent water leakage around the nails. Repair may entail resealing flashings, replacing a few shingles or tiles, or covering existing shingles with another layer of shingles. If a roof is already covered with several layers of shingles, adding another layer may not be an option. Instead, the roof will need to be stripped back to its decking and new tar paper and shingles, tiles, or metal applied.

Education and Training

Although not essential for all training programs, most require that trainees have a high school education or GED.

Thatched Roofs

Water reeds do not readily come to mind when American roofers think about roofing materials. But perhaps they should. Water reeds or Norfolk reeds are the preferred material used by roofers specializing in thatched roofs in Great Britain and the United States. Well-constructed and maintained thatched roofs can last for sixty years or longer—considerably longer than shingled roofs! Colin McGhee, a master thatcher, moved to the United States from England in 1992, after thatching the roof of a house in Virginia. His company now contracts to thatch everything from residential homes to buildings in zoos and theme parks. While working to establish a thatching school in the United States, McGhee teaches traditional thatching workshops at the Fox-Maple School of Traditional Building in Maine. If you want your roof thatched, Colin can be reached at Thatchit@aol.com.

High school courses that will be very helpful are English, mathematics, and drafting.

Many roofers have been trained while working as helpers for experienced roofers. This informal, on-the-job training includes putting up scaffolding on buildings and carrying equipment and roofing materials, as well as measuring, cutting, and fitting. After several months, trainees start to apply roofing materials. The experience and skills achieved are very dependent on the skill of the experienced roofer and the variety of roofing materials with which the roofer works.

Apprenticeship programs are an excellent way to learn the trade. Many are run by chapters of roofing unions. Programs usually run for three to four years. An apprentice spends a minimum of 2,000 hours on the job each year as well as 144 hours per year in the classroom. Apprentices are paid for their work.

Vocational and technical schools also offer training in roofing although these courses are usually part of an overall construction course.

Job Options

The Bureau of Labor Statistics reports that roofers hold about 158,000 jobs in the United States. Roofing jobs are not as affected by economic slowdowns as are other jobs in construction but may be seasonal in some parts of the country. New roofing techniques, tools, and materials have made individual roofers more efficient, so the total number of roofers needed on a particular job is not as great as it once was. This may restrict job growth in the industry to a small degree. About 25 percent of roofers are self-employed. Others work for roofing contractors, construction companies, or manufactured housing companies.

Learning About Roofing

Thanks to retired teacher, wrestling coach, and roofer Bobby Wilson, Ponca City, Oklahoma, has a win-win situation. Almost all of the members of the Ponca chapter of Habitat for Humanity, an organization dedicated to providing houses for low-income families, are retirees who spend two or three mornings a week helping to build Habitat houses. They have all developed building skills but, with a few exceptions, are not physically able to roof. This problem was solved when Wilson contacted Ponca's Pioneer Technology Center. The students in the center's construction technology course needed on-the-job training in roofing, and Habitat houses needed to be roofed.

With Wilson's supervision and moral support from other Habitat workers, students learned on the job and the houses got roofed!

Salary and Benefits

Data from the Bureau of Labor Statistics shows median weekly earnings for full-time roofers to be $363. Weekly salaries range from $210 to $711. The Chicago Roofers Union reports that the salary for members who are journeymen, or

Roofers repair Cincinnati's City Hall. Replicas of old shingles were made especially for this 1893 building.

experienced roofers is $28.15 per hour. Apprentices in their programs receive $14.08 per hour during their first year of training. They advance to $19.71 per hour during their fourth year of training. Benefit packages vary from employer to employer but are best for those in union jobs.

Pros and Cons

The availability of jobs, the stability of the job market, and good wages (at least in union jobs) are all positive aspects of roofing. Since no two roofs are exactly alike, roofers are challenged with each new job. Innovations in roofing materials

and techniques also provide challenges to roofers who want to stay current and competitive.

On the downside, roofing is physically demanding, requiring a lot of kneeling, twisting, and lifting. Since the workplace is many feet above ground level, there is risk of serious injuries from falls. In both 1999 and 2000, about one hundred workers died from injuries received on the job. There were 11,638 non-fatal job-related accidents to roofers reported to the Bureau of Labor Statistics in 1999.

FOR MORE INFORMATION

ASSOCIATIONS

Associated General Contractors of America
333 John Carlyle Street, Suite 200
Alexandria, VA 22314
(703) 548-3118
Web site: http://www.agc.org
This association is the voice of the American construction industry.

National Roofing Contractors Association
10255 W. Higgins Road, Suite 600
Rosemont, IL 60018
(847) 299-9070
Web site: http://www.nrca.net
One of the construction industry's oldest trade associations, NRCA is the voice of professional roofing contractors.

Roofing Contractors Association of British Columbia
9734 201st Street
Langley, BC V1M 3E8
Canada
(604) 882-9734
Web site: http://www.rcabc.org

United Union of Roofers, Waterproofers, and Allied Workers
1660 L Street NW, Suite 800
Washington, DC 20036
(202) 463-7663
Web site: http://www.unionroofers.com.
Contact this group for information on apprenticeship programs. For further information, e-mail bobk@unionroofers.com

WEB SITES

Bureau of Labor Statistics
http://www.bls.gov
This web site has an online handbook of occupations.

Peter Brugge Master Thatcher
http://www.thatching.net

ProConstruct.com
http://www.proconstruct.com

Roofing Contractor
http://www.roofingcontractor.com

BOOKS

Bolt, Steven. *Roofing the Right Way*. New York: McGraw-Hill, 1996.
This book gives good information on all aspects of roofing.

Brumbaugh, James, and John Leeke. *Complete Roofing Handbook*, 2nd ed. New York: McMillan, 1992.
This book has a section on roofing issues unique to historic homes.

Reid, Robert. *The Roofing and Cladding Systems Handbook: A Guide for Facility Managers*, 2nd ed. Englewood Cliffs. NJ: Prentice Hall, 1999.

Roofing and Siding. Menlo Park, CA: Sunset Books, 1994.
This is a good introductory book on roofing with many helpful do-it-yourself tips.

Schraff, Robert, and Terry Kennedy. *Roofing Handbook*, 2nd ed. New York: McGraw-Hill, 2001.
This is one of the bibles of roofing.

PERIODICALS
This Old House
AOL Time-Warner
(800) 898-7237
Web site: http://www.thisoldhouse.com

Professional Roofing
Published by National Roofing Construction Association, it is available by subscription.
Web site: http://www.nrca.net

Roofing Contractor/on line
Published by Roofer Business News Publishing Co.
Web site: http://www.roofingcontractor.com

VIDEOS
How-to Guide, Roofing (1993)
How-to Guide, Siding (1999)
Both of these videos were produced by Home Time Video.
http://www.hometime.com/store2/store.htm
Hometime Store
Attention: orders
4275 Norex Drive
Chaska, MN 55318
(888) 972-8453

5

LINEWORKER

Energy in the form of electrical power is essential to our modern way of life. Without it, most of us cannot heat or light our homes, cook our food, or have access to a myriad of other activities we feel are essential to our well-being. It is not until we are faced with a disaster like a tornado, a hurricane, or a severe ice storm that we realize how truly dependent we are on electrical power. Disasters also bring to our attention a group of people to whom we normally give little thought. In times of emergency they are our heroes. These are the men and women who work the lines to keep our electricity flowing.

Perhaps you enjoy working outdoors and are looking for a job that is interesting and challenging. If you enjoy the camaraderie of working on a team to complete difficult projects and can envision yourself out in all kinds of weather, then consider a career as a lineworker!

Job Description

The first job of a lineworker is to make sure that utility poles are stable. In the case of new construction or replacement of downed poles, new poles are set using machinery to dig the holes. Cranes are used to set the poles in place. When dealing with underground wires, a lineworker must be able to use trenchers, borers, and cable plows to prepare the ground to receive the wires.

The second step is to string cable along the poles or through conduits in the trenches. Lineworkers usually work from truck-mounted buckets when stringing cable to poles, but must be able to climb poles if necessary. Prior to stringing cable, insulators are clamped to the poles. The cable is then pulled by hand off huge reels and set in place on the insulators. The cable is tightened to the proper tension by hand and with hydraulic tools. Lineworkers also install

Winters are hard in North Pownal, Maine; winds blow down utility poles, trees fall across lines, and there are constant power outages. This employee from Central Maine Power gathers a downed line.

transformers, circuit breakers, switches, fuses, and other equipment to control and safeguard the lines.

Cable splicing is another facet of the job. Cable contains a number of wires. It is sometimes necessary to replace a segment of cable. This requires that the wires of the replaced segment be spliced, or connected, to existing wires of the cable. After splices have been made, insulation must be applied to the spliced areas before a moisture-proof cover is placed over the new segment of cable.

One of the biggest challenges of the job is troubleshooting. It is not always easy to locate a problem by looking at a cable. Using testing equipment, a lineworker identifies the source or cause of the problem and then develops and implements a plan to correct it. Lineworkers spend a portion of each day inspecting lines to identify those that would benefit from preventive maintenance.

Profile of a Lineman

A mini-interview with C. D. Thayer, powerline coordinator and long-time lineman.

WHAT DO YOU THINK ABOUT PRESENT APPRENTICE-SHIP PROGRAMS?

Thayer: From what I can see, I think they are doing an excellent job of providing the groundwork necessary to get a lineman started in linework.

DO YOU THINK THE FIFTEEN-WEEK PROGRAMS OFFERED IN SOME TECHNICAL SCHOOLS ARE HELPFUL OR ARE THEY REDUNDANT?

Thayer: I believe they are helpful.

HOW DID YOU GET YOUR TRAINING?

Thayer: I served a four-year apprenticeship at an electric cooperative to become a journeyman lineman, then went a step further and completed the IBEW (International Brotherhood of Electrical Workers) Journeyman Lineman exams.

DO YOU FORESEE PLENTY OF JOBS IN THE FUTURE IN LINEWORK?

Thayer: Yes. The 'nut twister' will be needed for as far as I can see, but they will use different tools, one of them being computers.

IF YOU HAD IT ALL TO DO AGAIN, WOULD YOU STILL BE A LINEMAN?

Thayer: Yes!

DO YOU HAVE ANY OTHER ADVICE FOR KIDS THINKING OF LINEWORK AS A CAREER?

Thayer: Yeah. For those boys and girls that enjoy doing something unusual to get a rush, they can get that in linework without breaking the law or hurting anyone. The potential for disaster is constantly present, but not so overbearing that you can't live with it for your entire career.

Education and Training

In the past, lineworkers were trained by working on the job with journeymen lineworkers. On-the-job training is still available in some companies, although most lineworkers are now trained in apprenticeship programs. Many receive four to six months of classroom work in a community college or a lineman-training center prior to starting their apprenticeships. Because they anticipate there will always be a need for well-trained lineworkers, the National Electric Contractors Association and the International Brotherhood of Electrical Workers formed the National Joint Apprenticeship and

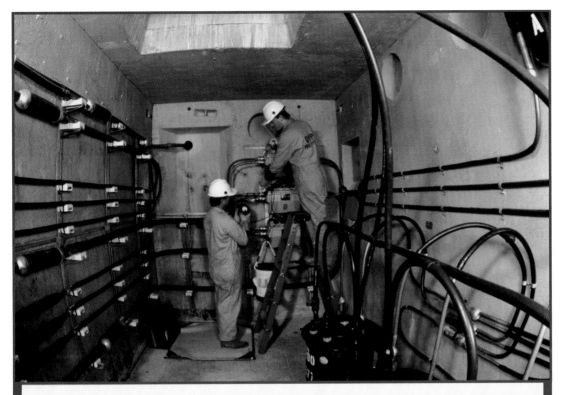

Because linework can be dangerous, future lineworkers undergo extensive training periods in facilities such as this one.

Training Committee, which developed the curriculum and the standards for apprenticeship training. To date, over 300,000 journeymen lineworkers have been trained in programs administered by NJATC. These programs require an applicant to be at least eighteen years of age, to have a high school diploma or GED, to have taken at least one year of high school algebra, to have a qualifying score on an aptitude test, and to be drug-free.

Apprenticeship programs administered by NJATC are usually run from three to four years, combining classroom work

Singing the Blues

Not many careers inspire composers and musicians to immortalize them in song. The plaintive melody and lyrics of "Wichita Lineman," composed and performed by Glen Campbell, tell the story of a lineman. The underlying theme is one of loneliness—perhaps a common feeling for many young people who carried the lines across the country and those who continue to service them in the out-of-the way places in this vast land.

with on-the-job training. Apprentices earn between 40 and 60 percent of the wages earned by a journeyman lineworker.

Job Options

The Bureau of Labor Statistics predicts that employment for lineworkers will continue to be good. Job opportunities are expected to increase by about 9 percent per year. This is due to growth in the telecommunications industry and the introduction of new technology. The demand for electricity has caused expansion of powerline networks, which also increases job opportunities. Lineworkers who are flexible and willing to move to new areas of the country will have the best chances for steady employment and rapid advancement to supervisory positions.

Salary and Benefits

Most apprentice lineworkers have starting salaries of $12 to $18 per hour. Journeymen lineworkers earn as much as $32 per hour. They also receive medical, dental, and life insurance, as well as pensions and 401(k) plans. This is a field in which overtime work is frequently necessary. Overtime may add as much as 15 percent to a worker's base salary.

Pros and Cons

When asked what he believes are the pros and cons of linework, C. D. Thayer, a powerline coordinator and long-time lineman said, "Biggest pro: a good dependable way to make a living and raise a family. Biggest con: A lot of stuff you do with high voltage isn't very forgiving and may not allow you a second chance."

FOR MORE INFORMATION

ASSOCIATIONS

International Brotherhood of Electrical Workers
1125 15th Street NW
Washington, DC 20005
(202) 833-7000

Web site: http://www.ibew.org
Here is the voice of electric workers throughout the United States and Canada. In addition to lobbying, this organization is also involved with apprenticeship programs and continuing education for its members.

National Association of Women in Construction
327 S. Adams Street
Fort Worth, TX 76104
(800) 552-3506
Web site: http://www.nawic.org
This organization was founded to enhance the success of women in construction, including the electrical industry.

National Electrical Contractors Association (NECA)
3 Bethesda Metro Center, Suite 1100
Bethesda, MD 20814
(301) 657-3110
Web site: http://www.necanet.org
Find an apprenticeship program for lineworkers through this association.

WEB SITES

The Electronic Lineman
http://www.E-lineman.com
This Web site is "where linemen and the internet collide." Lineworker jobs from around the world are listed here.

National Joint Apprenticeship and Training Committee
http://www.njatc.org
This Web site contains information about apprenticeship programs sponsored by IBEW and NECA.

Northwest Lineman College
http://www.lineman.com
This training center, located in Meridian, Idaho, is devoted to training lineworkers.

Oregon Tradeswomen, Inc.
http://www.tradeswomen.net
Here is a Web site that lists programs and other information for girls and women interested in non-traditional jobs in the trades. It also has a list of videos dealing with women in trades which can be borrowed.

Southeast Lineman Training Center
http://www.lineworker.com
Located in Georgia, this training center is devoted to training lineworkers.

BOOKS

Herman, Stephen L. *Delmar's Standard Textbook of Electricity*. Clifton Park, NY: Delmar Learning, 1998.
This book is considered to be the most comprehensive text about electricity on the market.

Kurtz, Edwin, et. al. *The Lineman's and Cableman's Handbook*. New York: McGraw-Hill, 1997.
This book is intended as an apprenticeship textbook as well as a home study resource.

Ryan, Charles. *Basic Electricity: A Self-Teaching Guide*. New York: John Wiley and Sons, 1986.
If you want to learn about electricity from scratch, you will find this book extremely useful.

Van Volkenburgh, Nooger. *Basic Electricity: Complete Course*, Volumes 1-5 in 1. Toronto: PROMPT Publications, 1997.
This is the bible on electricity for beginners.

PERIODICALS

EC&M (Electrical Construction and Maintenance)
Available by subscription.
Primedia Business Magazines
2104 Harvell Circle
Bellevue, NE 68005
Web site: http://www.primediabusiness.com

6

ELEVATOR CONSTRUCTOR AND REPAIRER

The year was 1852. The man was Elisha Graves Otis. The invention was one that would revolutionize the construction industry—the first safety elevator. Otis installed the first passenger elevator in a building in New York City in 1857, but it took the gearless traction elevator, developed and built by the Otis Elevator Company in 1903, to usher in the age of the high-rise building. Elevators are much more sophisticated today, with computer-controlled electronics, piped-in music, and subsonic speeds, but the basics have changed little since 1903.

People who build and install elevators are called elevator constructors. Besides installing new elevators, they maintain and repair existing elevators. Elevator constructors install and work on escalators, dumbwaiters, moving walkways, wheelchair lifts, and other similar equipment. They may also repair ski lifts!

Job Description

According to the *Occupational Handbook* of the U.S. Department of Labor, the first step in installing an elevator

The Flying Chair

King Louis XV of France owned the first elevator. It was built for him in 1743 and was known as the flying chair. The chair itself was located outside his palace, but the weights and pulleys that made it work were located inside one of the chimneys near his room. He entered his elevator from his balcony. Men stationed inside the chimney lowered him to the ground.

This elevator constructor fixes a grain elevator. Farmers must store grain through long winter months, and they rely on their machinery to work properly.

is to study building blueprints thoroughly to see what is needed to do the job. After the appropriate equipment and supplies have been assembled, elevator guide rails are bolted to the walls of the elevator shaft that has been constructed. Conduits to carry wires and controls are run up the walls of the shaft and secured in place. The wiring for the elevator is threaded through the conduits.

The next step is to assemble the elevator car, install it in the shaft on a steel frame, and attach guide shoes and rollers to prevent the car from rocking. Cables, drive wheels, and counterweights are added at the top of the elevator and attached to the electric power source, which is usually housed in an adjacent room. In some cases, elevators are operated by hydraulic plungers that push an elevator car

The Elevator Is a Star

The Otis elevator is one of the stars of the movie *Kate and Leopold* released in December 2001. Other stars of the show are Meg Ryan as Kate and Hugh Jackman as Leopold. Kate's ex-boyfriend, Stu, discovers a "portal" which allows him to be transported back in time. He journeys to New York City for the opening of the Brooklyn Bridge, which occurred in 1876. While there, he meets Leopold, third duke of Albany, a penniless Brit who has been sent to America to marry an American with money. Stu discovers that Leopold has invented a device, the elevator, which he has named Otis after his valet. Leopold is inadvertently transported back to 2001 with Stu. Before Stu can arrange to return Leopold to his own time, Stu falls down an elevator shaft and is hospitalized. He persuades Kate to look after Leopold. Needless to say, Kate and Leopold fall in love. Strangely enough all of the elevators in New York go on the blink when Leopold arrives and return to normal function when he travels back to 1876.

from beneath rather than pulling it by cables from above. When installation has been completed, the most skilled constructor in the crew, the adjuster, fine-tunes the controls so that the elevator works smoothly and efficiently.

For escalator installation, constructors build a steel framework, position the electrically powered stairs and tracts on which they run, and install associated wiring and motors.

Elevator maintenance and repair is done by constructors who specialize in repair work. Maintenance involves oiling and greasing moving parts, replacing worn parts, testing equipment with sophisticated instruments, and adjusting equipment for optimal performance. It is usually done on a schedule, as required by federal regulations. Repair work, especially if it involves replacing cables, doors, or machine bearings, may call for a service crew. These crews may also replace motors, hydraulic pumps, and control panels.

Education and Training

To be an elevator constructor trainee, you must be at least eighteen years old, have a high school diploma or GED, and pass an aptitude test. High school courses that will enhance your chances of being hired are algebra, geometry, physics, electricity, mechanical drawing, and basic computer skills.

Elevators have granted disabled men, women, and children a great deal of independence, allowing them to travel on public transportation and move freely through buildings.

With few exceptions, elevator constructors get their training in apprenticeship programs. Some are conducted by elevator manufacturing companies, but most have been developed and are administered by joint committees of employers and unions such as the National Elevator Industry Education Program (NEIEP). After a six-month probationary period, most trainees are accepted into a three- to four-year apprenticeship program that involves classroom work and on-the-job training. At the end of the apprenticeship, you must pass a standard mechanics exam to become a journeyman constructor. Most cities and states administer licensing exams that must be passed before a journeyman constructor can go to work.

NEIEP offers classroom training in one hundred locations across the United States. If a person does not live near any of the sites, support is offered via home study courses. NEIEP also sponsors continuing education programs for journeymen constructors.

Job Options

Data from the Bureau of Labor Statistics show that there are about 25,000 elevator constructors in the United States. Most work for special trade contractors, although elevator manufacturers and equipment companies also employ constructors. Because of the length of training programs and high salaries in the trade, most constructors stay in the business. There is little job turnover, so new journeymen constructors have to look hard for jobs. Those who specialize in maintenance and repair are more likely to find jobs than those who limit themselves to elevator installation alone.

Salary and Benefits

According to the Bureau of Labor Statistics, the median weekly salary for a non-union constructor is $844, with salaries ranging from $633 to $1,322. Union constructors make slightly more, with a median weekly salary of $865. Probationary workers receive about 50 percent of a journeyman's salary, or $432 per week. After completing the probationary period, an apprentice receives 70 percent of a journeyman's pay. Almost 80 percent of people working in the elevator industry are members of a union. This compares with 15 percent for all occupations and 23 percent for other craft and repair occupations. Union workers are more likely to have benefit packages than are non-union workers.

Pros and Cons

Elevator construction pays well. Usually done indoors, it is not often affected by weather extremes, and it has regular work hours. In maintenance and repair work, some overtime may be required, but this is minimal compared with many other repair jobs. It is, however, a trade in which it may be hard to find that first job.

It requires working in confined spaces in awkward positions and can be very strenuous. It also has some significant hazards including being hit or pinned by elevators, falling from heights, or sustaining electrical shocks. Like many trades dealing with electricity and electronics, there are many new innovations on the horizon. People willing to learn new techniques and master the use of computerized systems will do well in this field.

FOR MORE INFORMATION

ASSOCIATIONS

Elevator Conference of New York

150-17 12th Road
Whitestone, NY 11357-1809
(718) 767-5866
This organization is open to people interested in elevator safety, especially those in the vertical transportation business.

Elevator Escalator Safety Foundation

362 Pinehill Drive
Mobile, AL 36660-1715
(334) 479-2199
(888) RIDE-SAFE (743-3723)
Web site: http://www.eesf.org
Safety information about elevators and escalators can be found here.

International Union of Elevator Constructors

5565 Sterrett Place, Suite 310
Columbia, MD 21044
(410) 997-9000
Web site: http://www.iuec.org
Represents 80 percent of all people employed in the elevator industry.

Joint Apprentice and Training Committee

Office of Elevator Industry
386 Park Avenue South, Suite 301
New York, NY 10016-8804
(212) 689-0789
You'll find information here on apprenticeship programs.

National Elevator Industry Education Program

11 Larsen Way
Attleboro Falls, MA 02763
(800) 228-8220
Web site: http://www.neiep.org
This organization is dedicated to improving the knowledge and skill of helpers, apprentices and mechanics, to benefit them, their employers, and the trade. Look here for apprenticeship programs.

Women in Technology International

6345 Balboa Boulevard, Suite 257
Encino, CA 91316
(800) 334-WITI (9484)
Web site: http://www.witi.org
An organization dedicated to providing inspiration, education, online services, and publicity for women in technology.

WEB SITES

ApprenticeSearch.com

A Canadian web site listing apprenticeships.
http://www.apprenticesearch.com

National Elevator Industry, Inc.

http://www.neii.org

Otis Elevator Company

http://www.otis.com
On this site, you'll find good information on how elevators work as well as the history of the elevator.

BOOKS

Levine, Sy, and Jerry Worthing, eds. *Library of Basic Electricity*, vol. 1–3. Bountiful, UT: Electro-Horizon Publishing, 1987.

McCain, Zack. *Elevator Maintenance Manual*. Mobile, AL: Elevator World Inc., 1999.

Strakosch, George. *The Vertical Transportation Handbook*. New York: John Wiley and Sons, 1998.

The Guide to Elevating. Mobile, AL: Elevator World, Inc., 2002.

PERIODICALS

Elevator World
P.O. Box 6507
356 Morgan Avenue
Mobile, AL 36606
Web site: http://www.elevator-world.com
It is available by subscription.

VIDEOS

Elevator Safety Construction (1995)
Elevator Safety Repair (1995)
Safety While Installing Elevators (1995)
Web site: http://www.elevatorbooks.com
Electrical technician training videos developed by the National Association of Elevator Contractors.

7

HISTORIC PRESERVATIONIST

"Whoa!" you say. "How about those of us who prefer English to physics and art classes to electric shop? How about those of us who would rather go to a museum than a car rally? How about those of us who think that the Anasazi ruins at Mesa Verde or the buildings at Mount Vernon are more interesting than the international space station? What about us?"

Although restoring stained glass is a time-consuming process, the results are often breathtaking. This restoration artist cleans a stained glass window at St. Luke's United Methodist Church in Fairfield, Iowa.

A cool career without college may be harder for you to find. But it's not impossible! Take, for instance, the extremely cool career of historic preservationist.

Historic preservationists are people who work to protect historic landscapes (Civil War battlegrounds, for instance) and cultural and artistic properties that help us remember and understand our heritage. If you love history, enjoy sharing your enthusiasm for things historical with others, and are willing to learn many new skills, as well as revive some old ones, this career's for you!

Job Description

There is no single job description for this career. Historic preservationists find work in a variety of positions, and their duties are specific to the jobs they hold. For instance, a historic preservationist might be hired by a city or state agency that deals with historical buildings or restoration of historic districts. In this position, the preservationist would work with city planners, developers, architects, contractors, and others to help with the planning and implementation of the project. He or she would work with foundations and federal government agencies to get funding grants and would see that the restoration complied with regulations for historic buildings.

A historic preservationist might perch on a ledge in front of a south-facing cave in Arizona to figure out how to stabilize the walls of an ancient cliff dwelling. Or, like Carol Drake, a historic preservationist might work to preserve and restore the collection of a museum (see sidebar on page 76). Many preservationists find that their job descriptions change from day to day. They must be "jacks of many trades" and masters of them all. A very TALL order indeed!

Education and Training

Like the jobs themselves, the training of historic preservationists is also varied. Bucks County Community College in Newtown, Pennsylvania, lists the skills that a student in the

Preserving Graceland

Carol Drake, a 1996 graduate of Belmont Technical College's Building Preservation Technology Program was featured in an article in the January/February 1999 issue of *Magazine of Memphis Success*. The article by Lynn Conlee is entitled "All the King's Things" and deals with the team of preservation specialists who work at Elvis Presley's home, Graceland. Carol is a collections care specialist at Graceland and she, along with several others, is responsible for making sure that none of the King's things deteriorate whether "from aging, intrusive tourists or shipment to other museums and exhibits." The article, which can be reviewed on Belmont College's Web site, tells the story of how one person, trained as a historic preservationist, has used her training and skill for a really cool job in a REALLY cool place!

Historic Preservation Certificate program must attain before graduation. These skills are necessary to all preservationists, regardless of their mode of training.

A historic preservationist must understand the theoretical and historical basis of historic preservation, must demonstrate knowledge of the history of American architecture (or the architecture of the country in which he or she will be working), and must become familiar with research techniques to document historic sites. He or she must also be able to apply historic preservation standards to specific sites and, most of all, must be able to communicate historic preservation values to the general public.

Traditionally, preservation and conservation training in the United States has been by apprenticeship programs. Like all apprenticeships, skills are learned by working with those already trained and, in cases of lengthy apprenticeships, you earn while you learn. Hands-on training remains very important to all preservationists, but trade schools and college programs, especially at the graduate level, are the more common routes into this profession today.

The Colonial Williamsburg Foundation in Williamsburg, Virginia, is attempting to preserve the skills and techniques of eighteenth-century craftspeople by offering apprenticeships in thirteen of the craft shops in historic Williamsburg. Another purpose of the program is to provide skilled craftspeople to staff their shops for the educational benefit of those who visit Williamsburg. Apprentices for these programs must commit to spending five to six years training in the craft. While apprentices, they spend half of their time interpreting their skills to people. They explain the history and evolution of each craft to visitors from all over the world. At the end of their apprenticeships, most become career employees at Colonial

Craftspeople replace a floor using techniques from the seventeenth century. Like all the other residents of Colonial Williamsburg, they are wearing clothing from the same time period and appropriate to their jobs.

Williamsburg. The Colonial Williamsburg Foundation is their employer.

The National Park Service (NPS) sponsors a three-year apprenticeship through its Historic Preservation Training Center. Tom McGrath, director of the training center, says that many apprenticeships are available each year and are available to high school graduates as well as those with some training in preservation. He says that most of the trainees in this program have been or are employees of the park service. While it is not required that a person work for the National Park Service after completing the training, most apprentices are absorbed into full-time employment at one of the many historic sites of the NPS.

Several technical schools feature programs in historic preservation. Belmont Technical College in Ohio offers a two-year program leading to an associate degree in historic preservation that combines classroom work with work projects at historic sites. The Arkansas Institute of Building Preservation Trades offers two programs. The first is a one-year program that leads to a certificate of completion. The other is a two-year program leading to an associate of science degree. Both of these programs teach building techniques necessary to renovate, restore, and maintain historic buildings. Bucks County Community College in Pennsylvania also offers a historic preservation program.

Job Options

People with training in historic preservation are in demand by many employers in many different fields, so job opportunities are good. Jobs in museums, historic homes, and other agencies funded by grants from the federal government or from foundations may be influenced by the health of the economy, with fewer jobs being available in times of economic downturn. There is, however, growing interest in reevaluating and preserving our heritage. This will increase the demand for workers in this field.

Salary

Because of the variety of jobs within historic preservation, it is difficult to assess salaries. A job was recently posted in the Seattle area for a preservationist to work with the city government. The salary offered was $23.60 per hour. At Williamsburg, starting salaries for apprentices range from $9.00 to $12.00 per hour. After forty-five days, the apprentice is evaluated and there may be salary adjustments. A journeyman or master craftsman makes more than twice the salary of an apprentice. Depending on their educational background before their apprenticeships, exhibit specialists trained in restoration at the National Park Service are paid about $28,000 to $40,000 per year. Preservation specialists are paid about $28,000 to $34,000 per year.

Pros and Cons

The variety of job options is one of the positive features of this career. Depending on your interests, you can become a master craftsman, work in an office, preserve historic sites in many beautiful places in this country, or even work at Elvis's home, Graceland. You pick the job that works best for you. On the downside, you may have to work hard to find a training program that fits your goals. College-degree and even graduate-degree preservationists may be competing with you for jobs. The more credentials you have, the more employable you will be. This means you will need continuing education via workshops and seminars to stay competitive. The most interesting jobs in historic preservation may not be the best-paid jobs.

FOR MORE INFORMATION

ASSOCIATIONS

American Institute for Conservation of Historic and Artistic Works
1717 K Street NW, Suite 301
Washington, DC 20006
(202) 452-9545
Web site: http://aic.stanford.edu

Association for Preservation Technology International
4513 Lincoln Avenue, Suite 213
Lisle, IL 60532–1290
(888) 723-4242
Web site: http:// www.apti.org

Canadian Conservation Institute
Training and Information Division
Department of Communications
1030 Innes Road
Ottawa, ON K1A 0M5
Canada
(613) 998-3721
Web site: http://www.cci-icc.gc.ca

National Trust for Historic Preservation
Offices of Preservation
1785 Massachusetts Avenue NW
Washington, DC 20036
(202) 558-6000
Web site: http://www.nthp.org

TRAINING CENTERS

Arkansas Institute of Building Preservation Trades
1500 Tower Building, 323 Center Street
Little Rock, AR
(501) 324-9880
Web site: http://www.arkansaspreservation.org/aihbt
Offers courses in historic preservation.

Belmont Technical College
Preservation Department
120 Fox-Shannon Place
St. Clairsville, OH 43950
(740) 695-9500 ext. 4006
http://www.belmont.cc.oh.us/bpr/about.htm
This school offers courses in historic preservation.

Campbell Center for Historic Preservation Studies
203 E. Seminary Street
P.O. Box 66
Mt. Carroll, IL 61053
(815) 244-1173
Web site: http://www.campbellcenter.org
This center offers historic preservation studies in three- to five-day
seminars.

Colonial Williamsburg Foundation
Office of Human Resources
427 Franklin Street
Williamsburg, VA 23081
(800) History (447-8679)

Web site http://www.colonialwilliamsburg.org
Check this foundation for apprenticeships and employment at
Colonial Williamsburg.

Historic Preservation Training Center

4801A Urbana Pike
Frederick, MD 21704
(301) 663-8206
Web site: http:// www.nps.gov
Tom McGrath is the site manager of this National Park Service
training center.

WEB SITES

AntiqueRestorers.com

http://www.antiquerestorers.com
This online community of antique restorers provides information
and advice.

Preservation Resource Group

http://www.prginc.com

BOOKS

Burcaw, Ellis. *Introduction to Museum Work*, 3rd ed. Walnut Creek, CA:
Alta Mira Press, 1997.

Folson, Frank. *America's Ancient Treasures: Guide to Archeological Sites
and Museums*, 4th ed. Skokia, IL: Rand-McNally, 1993.

MacLeish, Bruce. *The Care of Antiques and Historical Collections*, 2nd ed.
Walnut Creek, CA: Alta Mira Press, 1985.

McGriffen, Robert. *Furniture Care and Conservation*, Revised 3rd ed.
Walnut Creek, CA: Alta Mira Press, 1992.

Praetzellis, Adrian. *Death by Theory: A Tale of Mystery and Archeological
Theory*. Walnut Creek, CA: Alta Mira Press, 2000.

8

MOTORCYCLE MECHANIC

In 1876, Nicolaus August Otto, a German engineer, invented the Otto cycle engine, the first practical alternative to the steam engine. Otto used his four-stroke internal combustion engine to construct a vehicle called the Otto Cycle. While this work was being done, one of Otto's young assistants, Gottlieb Daimler, was working on an engine of his own.

In 1885, Daimler attached his engine to a wooden bicycle and the motorcycle was born! In the century since that invention, motorcycles have changed dramatically and are now big business! Avid motorcyclists frequently work on their own bikes, but there is still demand for motorcycle mechanics with motorcycle manufacturing companies, dealerships, and on those occasions when bike owners would rather trust their bikes to service pros. If you love motorcycles and have good mechanical skills or are willing to learn them, you may have the makings of a first-rate motorcycle mechanic.

Job Description

The duties of a motorcycle mechanic fall into one of four categories: assembly, maintenance, repair, or restoration. Most of the time, motorcycles are shipped "broken down" from manufacturers to distributors. The pieces of the cycle must be reassembled before it can be sold. One of the duties of a motorcycle mechanic, especially an apprentice in the field, is to assemble the motorcycle using directions sent with the machine. Some helpers in motorcycle shops are specifically hired as assemblers and are not certified motorcycle mechanics.

Perhaps the biggest part of a motorcycle mechanic's time is spent in routine maintenance. This is especially true for

This Harley Davidson mechanic in Durango, Colorado, works on a customer's bike. Besides doing repairs, many motorcycle mechanics are asked to do custom modifications.

those who work for dealerships. Maintenance jobs include inspection and cleaning of brakes, electrical systems, fuel injection systems, plugs, carburetors, and other parts. Replacement of badly worn parts and adjustment of other components are included in maintenance regimens.

The big challenge for motorcycle mechanics comes when, in spite of good maintenance, a bike "just doesn't run right." To quickly diagnose the source of the problem requires that a mechanic use problem-solving skills and a lot of basic knowledge about motorcycles. Computerized diagnostic equipment can be used to help pinpoint the problem, but the mechanic's knowledge is the most important factor. Once the problem has been identified, the mechanic makes the necessary repairs. This may involve major overhaul of one or more of the systems on the bike or a simple tune-up. Mechanics who work on more than one make of motorcycle have to know the peculiarities of each make and model.

Many motorcycle mechanics, especially those who are self-employed, also repair motor scooters, mopeds, all-terrain vehicles (ATVs), and snowmobiles.

Education and Training

Although a high school diploma is not absolutely essential for someone to break into this field, formal training programs counselors and most employers prefer high school graduates or those with a GED. High school courses in English, electricity/electronics, math, small engine repair, and auto mechanics will be helpful. An after-school or summer job working in a motorcycle shop or dealership, or tinkering with your own bike will give you invaluable experience.

While many technical schools and community colleges provide courses in motorcycle repair, almost all motorcycle mechanics get some or all of their training on the job. Formal apprenticeships for motorcycle mechanics are much more

The Motorcycle Hall of Fame

The American Motorcyclist Association, through its American Motorcycle Heritage Foundation, has established the Motorcycle Hall of Fame. Like other such halls of fame, people compete for recognition, but here it's with their motorcycles. For many, the wonderful collection of classic machines featured in this museum is of much more interest than the over two hundred inventors, developers, and riders who are honored. Next time you are in Ohio, plan to visit this shrine to the motorcycle. It is located at 13515 Yarmouth Drive, Pinkerington, Ohio.

common in Canada than in the United States. Canadian programs require 5,400 hours of on-the-job training combined with classroom work before an apprentice is considered qualified to take written exams for a certificate of qualification.

The Motorcycle Mechanics Institute, one of the divisions of the Universal Technical Institute, is one of a small number of training facilities for motorcycle mechanics in the United States. It provides classroom work and hands-on experience in everything from basic engine theory to parts and dealership management. There are several other technical colleges across the country with similar programs.

Working on a racing motorcycle involves a lot of fine-tuning, as even the tiniest adjustments can give the rider an edge over the competition. Racing crews need to know how to work and think quickly.

Distance-learning programs are also available for those interested in motorcycle mechanics. There are several programs that supply instructional materials, basic tools, and knowledgeable instructors online or by phone. These programs provide the "book learning" but must be accompanied by some hands-on training.

The American Motorcycle Institute in Daytona Beach, Florida, offers advanced training in the repair of specific makes of motorcycles. Twenty weeks of training are offered for motorcycles from each of seven manufacturers: BMW,

Motorcycle Basics Online

For a really cool Web site, visit www.dansmc.com. Dan, the developer of the site, has been a motorcycle mechanic for over thirty-five years. He has his own repair shop in northern Idaho. This site features an absolutely free course in motorcycle repair that could easily be described as Motorcycle Repair for Dummies. The lessons range from the basics of two- and four-stroke engines to the more complicated concepts of motorcycle mechanics. They are easy to understand and are spiced with witty comments. Dan believes that one shouldn't spoil his or her love for motorcycles by choosing to repair them for a living. That said, he goes on to give a would-be motorcycle mechanic tips about how to become one. This Web site is a must-read for anyone with a yen for motorcycles.

Harley-Davidson, Honda, Kawasaki, Suzuki, Triumph, and Yamaha. These courses require that a participant already have the basic skills of a motorcycle mechanic.

Job Options

The Bureau of Labor Statistics forecasts that employment for motorcycle mechanics will increase slowly as the popularity of motorcycles rebounds. Motorcycle usage continues to be very popular with people between the ages of eighteen and twenty-four. It is making a big come-back with men over forty. Women are also showing an increasing interest in motorcycles. If oil, and therefore gasoline, shortages worsen, motorcycles may become even more popular than they are now, leading to a greater need for motorcycle mechanics.

Salary

The Bureau of Labor Statistics reports that the median annual salary for motorcycle mechanics is $25,000. The range of salaries is $15,980 to $41,180. For mechanics who work for dealers, the median annual salary is $25,650. In Canada, motorcycle mechanics earn Can$13 to Can$22 per hour.

Pros and Cons

Motorcycle mechanics are usually crazy about their jobs because they love motorcycles. Training can be obtained through correspondence courses, so you can learn at your own pace and still work at a regular job. People who work for manufacturers or dealers work regular hours in good working conditions.

Work may be seasonal, especially for those who are self-employed and living in northern states or Canada.

This may force mechanics to work on snowmobiles or other small-engine machinery.

The industry is affected by the economy. In times of economic slowdown, motorcycle mechanics may be subject to layoffs. The number of motorcycles brought for repair to a self-employed mechanic may decrease.

In the United States, formal training programs are often hard to find. With the advent of more technical schools across the country, this may improve.

FOR MORE INFORMATION

ASSOCIATIONS

American Motorcyclist Association
13515 Yarmouth Drive
Pickerington, OH 43147
(614) 856-1900
Web site: http://www.ama-cycle.org
The voice of 270,000 enthusiastic motorcyclists, this association was founded in 1924. It is dedicated to pursuing, protecting, and promoting the interests of motorcyclists.

Canadian Motorcycle Association
PO Box 448
Hamilton, ON L8L 1J4
Canada

(905) 522-5705
Web site: http://www.canmocycle.ca
Founded in 1946, this is the only national association for motorcyclists in Canada.

Women on Wheels Motorcycle Association (WOW)

P.O. Box 14180
St. Paul, MN 55114
(800) 322-1969
Web site: http:// www.womenonwheels.org
WOW represents over 3,500 women. Founded in 1982, its mission is to unite women motorcycle enthusiasts for recreation, education, mutual support, and recognition. It also promotes a positive image of motorcycling.

SCHOOLS

American Motorcycle Institute

3042 West International Speedway Boulevard
Daytona Beach, FL 32124
(800) 881-2264

Motorcycle Mechanic Institute (branch of Universal Technical Institute)

2844 West Dear Valley Road
Phoenix, AZ 85027
(800) 528–7995
        or
9751 Delegates Drive
Orlando, FL 32837
(800) 342–9253
Web site: http:// www.uticorp.com

WEB SITES

ApprenticeSearch.com

http://www.apprenticesearch.com
A Canadian site.

Durham Region Local Training Board
http://www.drltb.com

Professional Career Development Institute
http://www.pcdi-homestudy.com

Wisconsin Indianhead Technical College
http://www.witc.edu

BOOKS

Ash, Kevin. *BMW Motorcycles*. London: Carlton Books, 2001.

Coombs, Matthew. *Haynes Maintenance and Repair Manual for BMW 12850 and 1100 4-Valve Twins*. Pittsburgh, PA: Haynes Publishing, 1998.

Masi, Charles. *How To Set Up Your Motorcycle Workshop*. North Conway, NH: Whitehorse Press, 1998.

Raub, Nate, ed. *The Motorcycle Safety Foundation's Guide to Motorcycling Excellence*. North Conway, NH: Whitehorse Press, 1995.

Wilson, Hugo. *Motorcycle Owner's Manual*. New Conway, NH: Whitehorse Press, 1997.

PERIODICALS

Cycle World
Available by subscription or at newsstands.
Hachette Magazines
1633 Broadway
New York, NY 10019

Motorcycle Cruising
Motorcyclist Magazine
Published by Primedia Magazines, these titles are available by subscription or at newstands.
Web site: http://www.primediamags.com

HOROLOGIST

Horology is the age-old art and science of measuring time. The word "horology" is derived from two Greek words: *hora*, meaning "hour," and *legein*, meaning "to say or tell." Clockmakers, watchmakers, and repairers are called horologists. Although most people who fix things love to work with their hands, horologists must have high

Because horologists' performances are measured by the accuracy of the time pieces they work on, strict attention to detail is needed.

levels of manual dexterity and pay incredible attention to detail. Consider a career in horology if you love to tinker with tiny things!

Job Description

Horologists make repairs as simple as changing batteries in modern electrically powered quartz watches and clocks to fabricating tiny gears for antique timepieces. Since it is cheaper to replace moderately priced clocks and watches than to repair them, horologists spend most of their time working on expensive clocks and watches, many of which have mechanical movements and manual winding mechanisms or springs. This usually requires that a time-piece be dismantled and all parts cleaned and oiled. Components are inspected for excessive wear and, where necessary, they are replaced. For antique clocks and watches, a horologist may have to fabricate parts to complete a repair. The timepiece must be reassembled and adjusted to function accurately.

A horologist must be able to use metric measuring devices, be able to read and draw simple blueprints, and then be able to manufacture parts from the blueprints.

Education and Training

As with many trades, the traditional mode of education for horologists was by apprenticeship. Today, however, apprenticeships are very hard to arrange, and most horologists receive their education in technical or community colleges or in specialized programs dedicated to clock- and watch-making and repair. Several schools provide distance-learning programs using interactive Web sites, videos, or dedicated television classroom programs. Several master horologists have developed courses that incorporate textbooks and videos to teach the basics of clock and watch repair.

Most schools require that an applicant have a high school diploma or GED. They look for people with fine motor skills, good vision, and the ability to work alone with minimal supervision. High school courses that are helpful include English, basic math, blueprint reading, and machine shop.

Technical schools, or the technical branches of colleges or universities, offer courses leading to an associate of science or associate of applied science degree. An example of this is the course offered at the Okmulgee branch of Oklahoma State University. An associate of applied science degree is attained after satisfactory completion of 103 credit hours. An additional 24 hours of credit are available in advanced watch-making. OSU-Okmulgee is the only school in the United States to offer a university level watch-making course with 3,000 contact hours. This training is given under the supervision of the American branch of the Federation of the Swiss Watch Industry.

Believing that there is a very significant shortage of good horologists, the National Association of Watch and Clock Collectors (NAWCC) established the NAWCC School of Horology in 1995. Their course can be completed in fifty-six weeks and is broken down into eighteen units. Eight units deal with watch repair, and ten units cover clock repair. Graduates from this course can expect to attain at least an entry-level position in the horology industry.

What Is Horology?

Donn Lathrop, in an article entitled "What Is Horology?" found on the Web site of NAWCC, says that horology is "the science or art of measuring time." The concept of the sixty-second minute and the sixty-minute hour was proposed by scientists in ancient Babylonia. Time-keeping devices from the past include the sundial; water clocks, in which a bowl was either filled or emptied within a certain period of time; marked candles; and oil lamps that would burn a measured amount of oil. Early mechanical clocks were built by blacksmiths. The clocks had only one hand because they were so inaccurate that they could not measure minutes. Although Galileo understood the properties of the pendulum, Christian Huyghens was the first to apply them to clocks in 1673. After that, clocks became much more accurate, and time could be told to the minute. Further refinements in accuracy occurred when Lee Deforest invented the vacuum tube in the 1920s and the transistor in the 1940s.

The American Watchmakers-Clockmakers Institute (AWI) has also established a training program in horology. AWI's Academy of Watchmaking offers a 1,575-hour program that can be completed in forty-five weeks. The institute assists all full-time students in finding employment.

Job Options

The Bureau of Labor Statistics projects that employment for watch repairers will grow slowly. However, many people presently working in the field are approaching retirement age, which will leave many job opportunities for new horologists. The Federation of the Swiss Watch Industry projected that 25,000 new horologists will be needed worldwide by the year 2000. Of these, 10,000 will be needed in the United States alone. Another projection is that the number of horologists in the United States will decline by 32 percent by 2005 leaving a marked shortage of trained personnel in the field.

Many prestigious foreign watch/clock manufacturers have service centers in the United States. These centers provide the bulk of job opportunities for beginning-level horologists. Other horologists are employed in jewelry stores, in department stores that sell fine jewelry, or are self-employed. About 25 percent of horologists have their own businesses.

This horologer works carefully on an antique clock. It's common for older clocks to need custom-made parts fabricated from scratch. Some horologists collect old parts to use in repairs.

Salary

The median hourly wage for a watch repairer, according to the BLS, is $12.08. According to a survey by AWI, the median annual salary of a highly skilled horologist is $40,000.

Pros and Cons

This is a highly skilled trade in which a person works independently, with little supervision. Working conditions are usually excellent with good lighting, temperature control, and little noise. Job opportunities are good and should remain so for several more years.

A horologist must have superior manual dexterity and good eyesight. As we age, both of these physical attributes deteriorate. This may limit the length of one's career as a horologist. Formal training programs are still not plentiful, although distance-learning programs are becoming more common.

FOR MORE INFORMATION

ASSOCIATIONS

American Watchmakers-Clockmakers Institute (AWI)
701 Enterprise Drive
Harrison, OH 45030-1696
(513) 367-9800
Web site: http://www.awi-net.org
AWI is a non-profit trade association dedicated to the advancement of horology.

National Association of Watch and Clock Collectors, Inc.
514 Poplar Street
Columbia, PA 17512-2130
(717) 684-8261
Web site: http://www.nawcc.org

Time Service Department
U.S. Naval Observatory
3450 Massachusetts Avenue NW
Washington, DC 20392-5420
(202) 762-1467
One of the oldest scientific agencies in America, it is the preeminent authority in the area of timekeeping today.

SCHOOLS

The College of Instrument Technology
17156 Bellflower Boulevard
Bellflower, CA 90706
(310) 925-1785

Gem City College
School of Horology
7th and State Street
P.O. Box 179
Quincy, IL 62306
(217) 222-0391

Kilgore College
1100 Broadway
Kilgore, TX 75662
(903) 984-8531
Web site: http://www.kilgore.edu

The National Watchmaking School
1725 Boulevard du Carmel
Trois-Rivieres, PQ G8Z 3R8
Canada
(819) 691-3366

North Seattle Community College
9600 College Way North
Seattle, WA 98103
(206) 527–3600
Web site: http:// www.nsccux.sccd.ctc.edu

Oklahoma State University at Okmulgee
1801 E. 4th Street
Okmulgee, OK 74447-3901
(918) 756-621l ext. 266 or (800) 722-4471
Web site: http://www.osu-okmulgee.edu

BOOKS

Britten, F. *Horology Hints and Helps*. Wappinger Falls, NY: Antique Collectors Club, 1977.

Britten, F. *Old Clocks and Watches and Their Makers*, 6th ed. Wappinger Falls, NY: Antique Collectors Club, 1977.

Conover, Steven. *Clock Repair Basics*. Reading, PA: Clockmakers Newsletter, 1996.

Smith, Eric. *Clocks and Clock Repairing*. Cambridge, England: Lutterworth Press, 1993.

The History of Clocks and Watches. London: Orbis Publishing, 1979.

PERIODICALS

Chronos
This magazine is available by subscription.
Golden Bell Press
2403 Champa Street
Denver, CO 80205.
Web site: http://www.goldenbellpress.com

Clockmakers Newsletter
e-mail: sconover@ptdprolog.net.
Published by Steven Conover, it is available by subscription.

The Watch and Clock Review
This magazine is available by subscription.
Golden Bell Press
2403 Champa Street
Denver, CO 80205
Web site: http://www.goldenbellpress.com

10

HEATING, VENTILATION, AIR-CONDITIONING, AND REFRIGERATION (HVACR) TECHNICIAN

It doesn't take many 105-degree Fahrenheit (40.6° C) days in Dallas, or minus 20-degree Fahrenheit (-28.9° C) days in Duluth to help residents appreciate the skills of their favorite HVACR technicians. Climate control, at least control of the climate in our homes and workplaces, is becoming increasingly important. As the erratic effects of global warming increase, we need to protect ourselves by breathing cleaner, cooler air.

The $150 billion HVACR industry is the leader in climate control. And that's just here on Earth. Just think how important this industry will be when science fiction becomes fact and people begin to live in space stations, or on the Moon. If you want a career that offers job variety and stability, a good salary, and moving expenses to Mars, consider becoming an HVACR technician.

Job Description

HVACR systems are composites of mechanical devices connected by electrical wiring and a variety of pipes and ducts. They are controlled by sophisticated electronic systems, many of which incorporate computer technology. Technicians working on climate-control systems must be able to maintain the equipment and, when problems arise, be able to diagnose and repair the components that are no longer working properly.

Although they are trained to do both, technicians often specialize in equipment installation or maintenance and repair. Some specialize in one type of equipment, such as oil furnaces or solar panels. Most, however, are trained to work on a wide variety of equipment that enhances both job satisfaction and employment opportunities. Technicians must be able to install all the components of climate-control

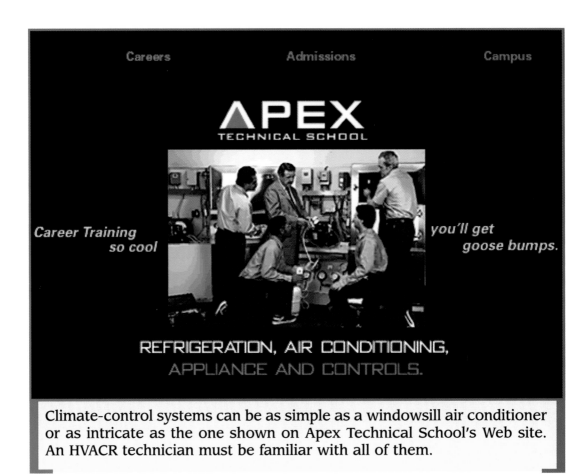

Climate-control systems can be as simple as a windowsill air conditioner or as intricate as the one shown on Apex Technical School's Web site. An HVACR technician must be familiar with all of them.

equipment by following blueprints, design specifications, and manufacturers' instructions. They must also be able to attach the equipment to pipes, ductwork, electrical power sources, and, in the case of air-conditioning systems, to refrigerant lines.

HVACR technicians usually work with sheet metal workers, plumbers, and electricians. Occasionally they must build ductwork and install electric and water lines themselves. People with experience or training in one or more of these areas, as well as in HVACR systems, are especially desirable employees.

Technicians who work with refrigeration and air-conditioning systems must be licensed by the Environmental Protection Agency (EPA) to work with refrigerants. Like chlorofluorocarbon and hydrochlorofluorocarbon, which leak into the atmosphere, refrigerants contribute heavily to the depletion of the ozone layer. Strict federal laws have been passed in an attempt to minimize further leakage of these chemicals into the environment. HVACR technicians must show that they are knowledgeable about refrigerant conservation, recovery, and recycling practices before they can work in the trade.

Education and Training

Heating, air-conditioning, and refrigeration systems are becoming more sophisticated by the day. Most employers are looking for people trained in technical schools and formal apprenticeship programs. A prerequisite for both of these training modalities is a high school diploma or GED. High school courses that will be very helpful in this trade are basic computer applications, computer-aided design, algebra and geometry, blueprint reading, mechanical drawing, sheet metal and electricity shop, basic business courses, and English. Communication skills are very important in this industry.

Many trade schools, technical and community colleges, and the military offer courses in HVACR. These may run for as little as six months. Training that lasts for two or more years leads to an associate of applied science degree. Aware of the need for an additional 20,000 HVACR technicians and installers each year, members from all branches of the industry have formed a coalition to develop and administer training programs to help increase the number of people who enter. These programs are apprenticeships that incorporate classroom studies with on-the-job training. Most of them are three- to four-year programs that allow apprentices to earn while they learn.

In addition to establishing apprenticeship programs with standard course work and training, members of the industry have also addressed the question of quality. Two certification programs have been developed to further the expertise of those working in the field. Certificates of excellence, earned by completion of these courses and passing of examinations, add to a technician's credentials and enhance the chances for advancement in this trade.

Job Options

The Bureau of Labor Statistics, as well as industry leaders, predict that job opportunities in the HVACR industry will continue to increase. In 2000, HVACR technicians and installers held 243,000 jobs in the United States. Industry leaders believe that over 20,000 new technicians will be needed every year to fill additional jobs and replace workers who are retiring or advancing to other jobs in the field.

Women as HVARC Technicians

Careers in the HVACR industry are considered non-traditional for women because more than 75 percent of workers in the field are men. An article featured in the summer 2000 issue of *Comfort Tech* and featured on the Cool Careers—Hot Jobs Web site, www.coolcareers.org, tells of a woman who is "Not Your Average Technician." Shanna Leeland, a college graduate with a degree in Russian linguistics, has chosen to pursue a career as an HVACR technician and she loves it. She chose the field because she thrives on challenge, likes working with her hands, and is a problem solver. She believes that women with HVACR training are appealing job candidates because they are adaptable, flexible, and can handle many tasks at once. When asked to describe her biggest challenge when in breaking into the HVACR field, she said, tongue in cheek, "My biggest challenge since joining this industry has been finding a proper bathroom."

About 35 percent of HVACR technicians work for heating and cooling contractors. Others work in industry, in schools and hospitals, for large shopping malls, in government buildings, and in a variety of other places where climate-control

systems exist. Twenty-five percent of HVACR technicians are self-employed.

Salary and Benefits

BLS data shows that the median average salary for HVACR technicians is $15.76 per hour. The range of salaries is $9.71 to $24.58 per hour. Beginning apprentices earn about 50 percent of the salary of experienced technicians. As they advance in their apprenticeships, they earn more. Most HVACR technicians also receive good benefit packages. This is especially true for those who are members of unions. About 20 percent of technicians in this field are union members.

Pros and Cons

Because good climate control improves quality of life, most people respect those who keep their furnaces and air conditioners working properly. One satisfaction that an HVACR technician derives from the job is knowing that people appreciate his or her work. Keeping climate-control systems in optimum working condition saves energy, helps

Large HVACR systems like this one require technicians to be physically agile and good at solving problems.

to produce a cleaner environment, and slows down the loss of stratospheric ozone. All of these things are critically necessary to insure that life remains livable and enjoyable on Earth. HVACR technicians have a variety of job possibilities—all of which pay well.

HVACR technicians do part of their work outdoors. As a result, bad weather may be a negative in this field. When working in buildings where heating or cooling equipment is being repaired, temperatures may be uncomfortable. Technicians frequently work in cramped or confined spaces and must squat, kneel, and twist to get to where they need to be. They may occasionally work in high places.

Electric shocks, burns, and cuts are hazards of the job as are frostbite and blindness for those who work with refrigerants. Appropriate safety equipment must be used to prevent refrigerant injuries.

FOR MORE INFORMATION

ASSOCIATIONS

Air Conditioning Contractors of America
2800 Shirlington Road, Suite 300
Arlington, VA 22206
(703) 575-4477

Web site: http://www.acca.org
The Air Conditioning Contractors of America help HVACR contractors to acquire, serve, and satisfy customers. Check this organization for training programs.

Air-Conditioning and Refrigeration Institute
4100 North Fairfax Drive, Suite 200
Arlington, VA 22203
(703) 524-8800
Web site: http://www.ari.org
Consult this group for training programs and competency exams. It's a national trade association representing manufacturers of more than 90 percent of all HVACR equipment in the United States.

Heating, Refrigeration, and Air Conditioning Institute of Canada
5045 Orbitor Drive, Building 11, Suite 300
Mississauga, ON L4W 4Y4
Canada
(800) 267-2231
Web site: http://www.hrai.ca
This institute represents HVACR manufacturers, wholesalers, and contractors in Canada.

Plumbing-Heating-Cooling Contractors Association (PHCC)
180 South Washington Street
P.O. Box 6808
Falls Church, VA 22040
(800) 533-7694
Web site: http://www.phccweb.org
This association has been the advocate of PHCC since 1883. It is the oldest trade organization in the construction industry.

Refrigeration Service Engineers Society
1666 Rand Road
Des Plaines, IL 60016-3552
(847) 297-6464
Web site: http://www.rses.org

This society has founded the RESE Technical Institute, a comprehensive course of study designed to assist members in attaining the highest level of competency in the HVACR industry.

WEB SITES

Cool Careers Hot Jobs
http://www.coolcareers.org
Launched in 2000 by a coalition of organizations in the HVACR industry, this Web site explains the industry's lifetime career benefits to students, parents, educators, counselors, and individuals looking for retraining. If you thoroughly investigate this site, you will have all the information you need to make a decision about pursuing a career in the HVACR industry. In addition, it contains a database of over 1,300 HVACR training schools and provides information on financial aid. Check it out!

BOOKS

Bobenhauser, William. *Simplified Design of HVAC Systems*. New York: John Wiley and Sons, 1994.

Mull, Thomas. *HVAC Principles and Applications Manual*. New York: McGraw-Hill, 1997.

Skimin, Gary. *Technicians Guide to HVAC Systems*. New York: McGraw-Hill,1995.

Swenson, Don. *HVAC Heating, Ventilatiing, and Air Conditioning*, 2nd ed. Hertfordshire, England: America Technical Publishers, 1992.

PERIODICALS

The Air Conditioning, Heating and Refrigeration News
Business News Publishers.
755 West Big Beaver Road, Suite 1000
Troy, MI 48084
(800) 837-8337
email: news@omeda.com

11

COMPUTER REPAIR TECHNICIAN

Throughout history, certain machines have revolutionized the world. Alexander Graham Bell's telephone, Henry Ford's automobile, and the Wright brothers' airplane are some of the inventions that helped to shape life as we know it today. No invention, however, has had greater impact on our lives than the computer! In less

than sixty years, its use has pervaded almost every aspect of our lives.

There are now over 100 million computers in use in the United States alone, and 50,000 more are being purchased daily! Who takes care of all these computers? Computer repair technicians do. The demand for well-trained computer technicians is far greater than the supply, so give this career serious consideration!

Job Description

Computer repair technicians have three main responsibilities. They install or set up computers and peripheral equipment, such as printers and scanners; they provide ongoing maintenance for the machinery; and they make repairs. Technicians provide hands-on service. People who provide technical assistance, usually by phone, to computer system users are known as computer support specialists and have different training and responsibilities than do computer technicians.

The installation of large equipment like mainframe computers requires that technicians connect the equipment to

This computer repair technician solders components on a circuit board. Because it is so complex, computer hardware must be carefully maintained.

Computers for Schools

The Miami-Dade Community College Computer Technician Program not only teaches students basic computer theory and repair techniques, but also offers them the chance to participate in a program called Computers for Schools. Students work as apprentice technicians to build new computers or refurbish used computers to be given to schools and school children throughout Florida. The practical experience provided to apprentice technicians through this program is very valuable when they are ready to apply for jobs.

power sources and communication lines. Technicians who install operating software and peripheral equipment must be sure all equipment is configured to function correctly and efficiently. In some cases, technicians may also install personal computers, although this is usually handled by the purchaser.

Computer technicians who travel to customers to do maintenance or repair work are called field technicians. Those who work for specific computer manufacturers may work in a particular area of the country and make regular visits to companies or institutions that use their computers. They provide routine maintenance and are on call for emergency repairs. Field technicians usually make repairs by replacing components such as video cards, hard drives, or network cards. These components are relatively inexpensive and can be replaced quickly so a company's computers are not down for any length of time.

Defective components are returned to service centers where they are examined by bench technicians who use sophisticated diagnostic equipment to pinpoint problems. If possible, bench technicians repair the component parts. Bench technicians also work on personal computers and peripheral computer equipment that customers bring to their shops or service centers. Again, diagnostic software is used to help define problems, then appropriate repairs are made.

Education and Training

High school students often elect computer courses as part of their secondary school education. Almost all high schools have at least some basic computer courses to whet the appetites of future computer technicians. Not long ago, the computer industry was most interested in hiring people as programmers. Today the shortage in the industry lies in the technology of installation, maintenance, and repair.

Besides basic computer classes, high school students should consider courses in electricity/electronics, algebra and geometry, as well as communication skills. Computer technicians will work with many customers who have only rudimentary knowledge of simple computers. Technicians

Computer technicians must be detail oriented, as even one mistake can result in the loss of someone's data. Dust and electrical surges also cause havoc with computer components.

must be able to explain clearly what the problems are and what must be done to correct them.

Computer repair technicians are trained in technical schools, community colleges, in programs set up by manufacturers, or by distance-learning courses taught by colleges or private companies. School programs vary in length. Some, which can be finished within nine months, lead to a certificate of completion. Others, which may be as long as two years, may grant an associate of science degree. All of these programs include courses in computer theory as well as hands-on training. (See sidebar on page 120.)

Computers and Punch Cards

What do the textile industry and the computer industry have in common? The Jacquard loom, named for Joseph-Marie Jacquard who invented it in 1820, uses a series of punch cards to control the patterns that are woven into cloth by looms. In 1832, Charles Babbage, an English mathematician who is one of the fathers of modern computers, "borrowed" the idea of punch cards from the Jacquard loom. He used them to put operation instructions into his analytical machine. Although this machine was never produced for commercial use, the concepts behind it formed the basis for today's computers. Herman Hollerith also applied Jacquard loom concepts to computers. He used punch cards to store data which he later fed into machines to compile the results of the 1889 United States Census. Punch cards are still used for similar purposes in the computer industry today.

Regardless of training, entry-level computer repair technicians will enhance their employability if they earn an A+ certificate. A+ certification is a testing program for entry-level technicians. It is administered by the Computing Technology Industry Association (ComTIA). This association represents over fifty major computer hardware and software vendors, distributors, and others concerned about the quality of computer service. Obtaining an A+ certificate tells employers and customers that a technician has the knowledge and ability to do basic computer repair.

Job Options

The Bureau of Labor Statistics says that opportunities for computer repair technicians should be excellent. Employers report difficulty finding qualified applicants. With huge numbers of new computers being purchased daily, mostly by people who lack the ability to make computer repairs, the shortage of computer technicians continues to grow rapidly. Many people buy computers online rather than from local distributors. These people rely heavily on local repair shops for computer maintenance and repair.

Salary

The median hourly wage for computer technicians, according to the BLS, is $15.08, with a range of $9.50 to $23.42. Since the supply of highly skilled technicians does not meet the demand for their services, salaries may be much higher in areas of the country where there are few technicians. Yearly income may be augmented by overtime work.

Pros and Cons

Jobs in computer technology are plentiful, salaries are high, and one need not spend large amounts of time in training to gain the basic skills necessary for entry-level positions. Since computer components are affected by extremes in temperature, work is usually done in shops with good climate control, good lighting, and pleasant surroundings.

Technicians who work for companies that supply large numbers of computers to businesses may be required to work long hours, usually after the business work day. They may have to travel long distances and may be on call for emergency repairs.

FOR MORE INFORMATION

ASSOCIATIONS

Association of Computer Support Specialists
218 Huntington Road
Bridgeport, CT 06608
(203) 332-1524
Web site: http:// www.acss.org
Seeking to promote recognition of computer support as a profession, this group encourages people to use education and personal contacts

to advance their careers. Association members include help-desk specialists, computer repair technicians, network engineers, and others.

Association for Women in Computing
41 Sutter Street, Suite 1006
San Francisco, CA 94104
(415) 905-4663
Web site: http:// www.awc-hq.org
Dedicated to the advancement of women in technical fields, this is a professional organization for women who are interested in information technology.

Canadian Information Processing Society
2800 Skymark Avenue, Suite 402
Mississauga, ON L4W 5A6
Canada
(905) 602-1370
Web site: http://www.cips.ca
Founded in 1958, the society represents over 8,000 Canadian information technologists.

Computing Technology Industry Association
1815 South Meyers Road, Suite 300
Oakbrook Terrace, IL 60181-5228
(630) 268-1818
Web site: http:// www.comptia.org
This association develops and administers certification programs.

WEB SITES

Computer Training Schools
http://www.computer-training-schools.com
If you are considering a career in computer technology, this Web site is a must. It lists schools throughout the country that offer courses in computer repair. The Web site is dedicated to helping students find classes in computer training.

Foley-Belsaw Institute
http://www.foley-belsaw.com
This institute offers home study courses for many careers including computer repair.

National Association of Career Colleges (Canada)
http://www.nacc.ca/schools.htm
Listing career schools in Canada by province and city, this site includes brief overviews of the courses of study offered by each.

National Institute of Technology
http://www.nitschools.com
This site features the nine institute campuses, highlighting their programs which include computer repair.

BOOKS

Bigelow, Stephen. *PC Technicians Troubleshooting Pocket Reference*, 2nd ed. New York: McGraw-Hill, 2000.

Meyers, Michael. *A+ All-in-One Certification Exam Guide*. New York: Osborne McGraw-Hill, 2001.

Mueller, Scott. *Upgrading and Repairing PCs*, 14th ed. Indianapolis, IN: Que Publishing, 2001.

Soper, Mark, and Scott Mueller. *Upgrading and Repairing PCs: A+ Certificate Guide*. Indianapolis, IN: Que Publishing, 2001.

White, Ron, and Timothy Down. *How Computers Work*. Indianapolis, IN: Que Publishing, 2001.

PERIODICALS

Maximum PC
Web site: http://www.futurenetworkusa.com/
Published by Future Network, U.S.A., *Maximum PC* is available by subscription and at newstands.

12

UPHOLSTERER

Are you a furniture freak? Do you keep an eye out for that unusual chair or funky footstool at flea markets or garage sales? Do your closets bulge with fabric that you've bought at half-price sales—just because you liked it? If you fit this description and are manually dexterous, you have the makings of a first-class upholsterer. As many upholsterers are reaching retirement age, the job market for upholsterers is starting to open up. Give serious thought to this cool career.

Job Description

The first step may be the most difficult. It is to decide, or help your client decide, what fabric to use in a reupholstery job. Once that decision is made, you remove the old fabric and stuffing from the piece of furniture until you reach the springs and frame. The frame is inspected for any damage. If the frame is wooden, it may be necessary to reglue parts of the frame or otherwise stabilize the damage. Metal frames may need to be rewelded. The webbing that is affixed to the frame will frequently need to be replaced in order to support the springs.

The springs are then retied or replaced before being covered with a filler of foam rubber or polyester batting.

Once the underpinnings are secure, the fabric which has been chosen is measured and cut, and the pieces are sewn together. The fabric is then stretched over the foam rubber or batting and secured to the frame with tacks, staples, nails, or glue. Ornaments such as fringe or buttons are then applied to finish the piece.

Upholsterers may also work on car, truck, boat, and airplane seats. They may repair or replace awnings, sail covers, tents, and other canvas structures.

This upholsterer is repairing an older or secondhand piece of furniture. Fresh fabric, chosen by the client, will give this chair a new life.

Education and Training

A high school education is strongly recommended for those who plan to be upholsterers. Courses that will be very helpful are English, business, woodworking, math, and sewing. Yes, guys, you too can learn the basics of sewing in high school if this career appeals to you! Your high school may offer basic upholstering courses that will get you off to a great start.

After high school, you may want to take additional upholstering courses offered at a community college or trade school near you. These courses are sometimes offered at night, so you can take them and still work at your survival job full-time.

Distance-learning courses are available through several colleges. In addition, several companies provide video instructions and textbooks that give step-by-step guidance to reupholstering different types of furniture. This mode of learning requires that you have the self-discipline to do the work without an instructor looking over your shoulder.

The International School of Upholstery in Portland, Oregon, offers three programs. The first is a six-month apprenticeship that teaches the basics. Twelve- and twenty-four-month programs are also available. The additional skills learned in the longer programs enhance credentials for employment. Beyond upholstery skills, wood construction and repair is emphasized in the longer programs. This is especially helpful if you plan to work in the antique restoration business.

Craft schools teach upholstery along with wood refinishing. Many of these are located in parts of the country traditionally known for craft work, such as North Carolina, which is home to a large number of furniture manufacturers.

Seminars and short courses are available through the Smithsonian Institute and other world-class museums. Most of these courses, which require that you have basic upholstery skills, are geared to people who want to pursue furniture restoration as a career.

Although they are difficult to find, some experienced upholsterers will accept students who wish to learn on the job. Most of these apprenticeships are informal, requiring

Fabric Made From Oil

What do your gas grill and your favorite couch have in common? The answer is oil. The connection of oil to your gas grill is obvious. Everyone knows that the propane used to power the grill and cook your hamburgers is one of the many fuels refined from crude oil. What you may not know, however, is that the polyester batting inside your couch and the fabric covering it are also made from oil. In 1931, Wallace Carothers, an American chemist working for the DuPont Company, reported on the development of a new fiber made from giant molecules called polymers. The fiber he developed was identified as "66" because of its molecular structure, but is better known today as nylon. Nylon was synthesized from oil-based products called petrochemicals. Its development led to the manufacture of an amazing array of new synthetic fibers including the polyester batting in your couch and the fabric that covers it.

about three years before the apprentice is ready to work on his or her own. This traditional way of learning the trade is relatively uncommon today.

Job Options

The Bureau of Labor Statistics reports that there were about 58,000 upholsterers working in the United States in 2000, 25 percent of whom were self-employed. Other upholsterers work for furniture manufacturers, auto repair shops, airlines, interior decorating firms, and large upholstery shops. In addition to their upholstery jobs, many experienced upholsterers teach part-time at technical schools or colleges.

Job opportunities in this trade have been negatively influenced by improvements in the durability and soil resistance of furniture and automobile seat fabrics. In many cases, it is cheaper to buy new furniture than to refinish older pieces. Because of this, few young people have trained as upholsterers in the last several years. Many upholsterers are fast approaching retirement age. As a result, there is now a relative shortage of trained upholsterers. This means that job availability should improve in the near future. There will always be jobs for skilled upholsterers who can restore expensive furniture and antiques.

Salary

The Bureau of Labor Statistics reports that the median hourly wage for upholsterers is $11.42 per hour. No data is available for those who are self-employed, because earnings are dependent on many factors, including the numbers of

Upholsterers don't only work on furniture. In York, northern England, this upholsterer is assembling a train seat.

hours worked, the affluence of the area in which a person is working, and the business acumen of the upholsterer.

Pros and Cons

You can obtain upholstery skills in many ways. The basic equipment, which is minimal, is available in most hardware stores. Jobs can be found in a variety of places, from museums to airlines. Or, you may choose to work for yourself. There is a lot of satisfaction in making a beautiful reupholstered piece emerge from a dilapidated, thrift-shop reject.

The job, which can be strenuous, requires a considerable amount of stooping and bending. Some of the furniture on which you work may be quite heavy. If you use leather or canvas, a considerable amount of strength may be needed to handle the materials. While most work is done indoors in climate controlled, well-ventilated shops, there may be debris and fumes from batting, fabric, or glue that can cause lung irritation. Hand injuries caused by broken frames or springs, sharp tools, and nails or tacks are not uncommon. It is necessary to wear gloves and protective eyeglasses on occasion. The trade is affected by the economic climate.

FOR MORE INFORMATION

SCHOOLS

Foley-Belsaw Institute
6301 Equitable Road
Kansas City, MO 64120
(800) 821-3452
Web site: http://www.foley-belsaw.com
This institute offers many home-study courses that incorporate videos, text books, and technical assistance by phone. They also provide basic equipment needed to get started in the trade.

International School of Upholstery
9700 NW Cornell Road
Portland, OR 97229

(888) 292-2053
Web site: http://www.upholsteryschool.com
This school offers courses which last from six to twenty-four months.

WEB SITES

Upholster Magazine Online
http://www.upholster.com
This Web site offers six training videos that cover everything from upholstery basics to starting and operating an upholstery business.

World Wide Learn
http://www.worldwidelearn.com
This Canadian Web site is the world's largest online directory of colleges, courses, degrees, programs, learning resources, and education opportunities in sixty-nine subjects.

BOOKS

Gheen, Lloyd. *Upholstery Techniques*. New York: McGraw-Hill, 1994.

James, David. *The Upholsterer's Pocket Reference Book: Materials, Measurements, Calculations*. London: Sterling Publications, 1995.

Furniture Finishing and Refinishing. Menlo Park, CA: Sunset Publishing, 1990.

Furniture Upholstery. Menlo Park, CA: Sunset Publishing, 1988.

Slipcovers and Bedspreads. Menlo Park, CA: Sunset Publishing, 1994.

VIDEOS

Merv's Work at Home Training Course
N2758 Shadow Road
Waupaca, WI 54981-9497
Merv has produced a series of videotapes based on his forty years as an upholsterer. The basic course, entitled *Merv's Upholstery Training* is a set of two, three-hour long videos. He also has two other videos entitled *Merv's Upholstery Secrets* and *Merv's Upholstery Repair*.

GLOSSARY

apprentice A person who, under the supervision of a skilled worker, is learning a trade by practical experience.

Babylonia An ancient city-state in what is today Iraq.

batting Sheets of cotton, wool, or synthetic fiber used as the filler in quilts or for padding over the frame of a piece of furniture.

Bureau of Labor Statistics (BLS) An agency of the Department of

Labor of the United States federal government that compiles statistics about the labor market.

camaraderie The goodwill that exists between coworkers and friends.

carbon fiber A sturdy polymer made from the carbon-containing materials left over after the refining of crude oil. Items made from it are lightweight and very strong.

Carborundum A brand name for certain abrasive materials.

conduit A tube or trough for receiving and protecting electric wires or cables.

dexterous Skillful, especially when using one's hands.

diagnosis The art or act of identifying a problem based on signs or symptoms.

distance learning A form of education in which the student is not in direct physical proximity to the teacher. Examples are correspondence courses, Internet education programs, and radio-telephone or closed-circuit TV courses.

facet A phase or aspect.

gender Pertaining to being male or female.

global warming The increase in average or mean temperature throughout the world due to the larger amount of carbon dioxide and other greenhouse gases that have been released into the atmosphere.

jargon The technical language of a trade, a profession, or of science.

journeyman An experienced worker who has learned a craft or trade, as opposed to an apprentice who is still learning the trade.

kiln A large, very hot oven used for hardening, or drying, materials such as clay or glaze.

linguistics The study of languages.

mason A person who builds with stone, brick, or concrete.

plaintive Expressing sorrow or melancholy.

refrigerant Chemical substances used to create the cooling effects of refrigerators or air-conditioning units.

scaffold A temporary platform to hold workers and tools during the construction or repair of a building.

self-employed Earning income directly from one's own business, trade, or profession.

silica Silicon dioxide; quartz and opal are forms of silica.

thatch A roof covering made of straw, rushes, reeds, or leaves.

trowel Hand implement used to spread or smooth loose material such as concrete.

INDEX

A

American Motorcycle Institute, 89

American Watchmakers-Clockmakers
     Institute, 99–100, 102

apprenticeship, 8, 13, 35, 37, 46, 48, 55,
     56–58, 67, 69, 77–78, 80, 85, 87–88, 97,
     109, 110, 113, 120, 131–132

Arkansas Institute of Building Preservation
     Trades, 79

associates degree, 12, 23, 79, 98, 110, 122

auto body repair technician
     education/training for, 11–13
     job description, 11
     job options, 13–15
     pros/cons of, 15–16
     qualities needed to be, 10

resources for, 16–18
salary/benefits, 15
Automotive Service Association,
 9–10
aviation technologist
 education/training for, 22–23
 job description, 20–22
 job options, 24–25
 pros/cons of, 26–27
 resources for, 27–29
 salary/benefits, 25–26
 specialties of, 21
avionics, advances in, 24

B
Belmont Technical College, 76, 79
Bucks County Community
 College, 75–76, 79
Bureau of Labor Statistics (BLS),
 14, 15, 35, 37, 46, 47, 49,
 58, 68, 90, 91, 100, 102,
 110, 113, 124, 133

C
cement, 30, 31–33, 34
certification/licensing, 12, 13, 23,
 68, 76, 79, 85, 88, 109, 110,
 122, 123–124
Chicago Roofers Union, 47
Colonial Williamsburg
 Foundation, 77–78, 80
community college, 8, 12, 14, 56,
 75, 87, 97, 109, 120, 122, 130
computer repair technician
 education/training for, 121–124
 job description, 119–121

job options, 124
pros/cons of, 125
resources for, 125–127
salary, 124
Computing Technology Industry
 Association (ComTIA),
 123–124
concrete mason
 education/training for, 35
 job description, 33–34
 job options, 35–36
 pros/cons of, 37–38
 resources for, 38–40
 salary/benefits, 37

D
Department of Labor, 14, 20, 63
distance-learning program, 8, 89,
 91, 97, 102, 122, 131
Drake, Carol, 75, 76

E
elevator constructor and repairer
 education/training for, 66–68
 job description, 63–66
 job options, 68
 pros/cons, 69
 resources for, 70–72
 salary/benefits, 68–69
Environmental Protection Agency
 (EPA), 109

F
Federal Aviation Administration
 (FAA), 19–20, 21, 22–23,
 24, 25

Federation of the Swiss Watch
    Industry, 98, 100
Fell, Diana, 14
flying chair, 63
Fox-Maple School of Traditional
    Building, 45

G
GED (general equivalency
    diploma), 8, 12, 22, 35, 44,
    57, 66, 87, 98, 109
Graceland, 76, 80

H
Habitat for Humanity, 47
historic preservationist
    education/training for, 75–79
    job description, 75
    job options, 79
    pros/cons of, 80–81
    resources for, 81–83
    salary, 80
home study, 8, 68
horologist
    education/training for, 97–100
    job description, 96–97
    job options, 100
    pros/cons of, 102
    qualities needed to be, 95–96,
        98, 102
    resources for, 103–105
    salary, 102
horology, defined, 99
HVACR technician
    education/training for, 109
    job description, 107–109

job options, 110–113
pros/cons of, 113–114
resources for, 114–116
salary/benefits, 113
women as, 111

I
I-Car Education Foundation, 13, 15
International Brotherhood of
    Electrical Workers, 55, 56
International School of
    Upholstery, 131

L
Leeland, Shanna, 111
lineworker
    education/training for,
        56–58
    job description, 53–55
    job options, 58
    profile of a, 55–56
    pros/cons of, 59
    resources for, 59–61
    salary/benefits, 59

M
McGhee, Colin, 45
McGrath, Tom, 78
Miami-Dade Community
    College, 120
Motorcycle Hall of Fame, 88
motorcycle mechanic
    education/training for, 87–90
    job description, 85–87
    job options, 90
    pros/cons of, 91–92

resources for, 90, 92–94
salary, 91
Motorcycle Mechanics Institute, 88
museums, 73, 79, 131, 134

N
National Association of Watch
    and Clock Collectors,
    98, 99
National Electric Contractors
    Association, 56
National Elevator Industry
    Educational Program, 67, 68
National Institute for Automotive
    Service Excellence, 13
National Joint Apprenticeship and
    Training Committee, 56–57
National Park Service, 78–79, 80

O
Occupational Handbook, 20, 63
on-the-job training, 13, 23, 35, 45,
    47, 56, 58, 67, 87, 88, 110
Otis Elevator Company, 62, 65

P
punch cards, 123

R
refrigerants, 109, 114
roofer
    education/training for, 44–46
    job description, 43–44
    job options, 46
    pros/cons of, 48–49

resources for, 49–51
salary/benefits, 47–48

S
Smithsonian Institute, 131
Spartan School of Aeronautics, 24

T
technical/vocational school, 8,
    11, 12, 14, 23, 46, 55, 79, 87,
    88, 92, 97, 109, 122, 133
thatched roofs, 45
Thayer, C. D., 55, 59
trade school, 8, 12, 14, 77, 98, 130
training, types of, 14

U
unions, 37, 47, 48, 67, 68–69, 113
Universal Technical Institute, 88
upholsterer
    education/training for,
        130–132
    job description, 129
    job options, 133
    pros/cons of, 133
    resources for, 135–136
    salary, 133

V
Vineyard, Gene, 35–36, 37

W
Wilson, Bobby, 47
women, 8, 111
Wright, Orville and Wilbur, 19, 117

About the Author

Linda Bickerstaff, M.D., writes from her home in Ponca City, Oklahoma.

Photo Credits

Cover © Mark Segal/Index Stock Imagery, Inc.; pp. 9, 10 © Kent Dufault/Index Stock Imagery, Inc.; p. 12 © Richard Hamilton Smith/Corbis; pp. 19, 20 © Tim Wright/Corbis; p. 22 © Richard T. Nowitz/Corbis; pp. 30, 32 © Gary Moon/Index Stock Imagery, Inc.; p. 36 © Jim A. Sugar/Corbis; pp. 41, 42 © James H. Pickerell/The Image Works; p. 48 © Al Behrman/AP/Wide World Photos; pp. 52, 54 © Robert F. Bukaty/AP/Wide World Photos; p. 57 © Roger Ressmeyer/Corbis; pp. 62, 64 © Kevin Beebe/Index Stock Imagery,Inc; p. 67 © Philip Kaake/Corbis; pp. 73, 74 © Dave Kettering/*Telegraph Herald*/AP/Wide World Photos; p. 78 © Michael Geissinger/The Image Works; pp. 84, 86 © Nancy Richmond/The Image Works; p. 89 © Shuji Kajiyama/AP/Wide World Photos; pp. 95, 96 © Steve Prezant/Corbis; p. 101 © Omni Photo Communications Inc./Index Stock Imagery, Inc.; pp. 106, 112 © James A. D'Addio/Corbis; p. 108 courtesy of Apex Technical School; pp. 117, 118 © Steve Niedorf Photography/The Image Bank; p. 122 © Bill Miles/Corbis; pp. 128, 130 © William Taufic/Corbis; p. 134 © Collin Garratt/Milepost 92 1/2/Corbis.

Design and Layout

Evelyn Horovicz